Anonymous

The Empire of Brazil at the World's Industrial and Cotton Centennial Exposition of New Orleans

Anonymous

The Empire of Brazil at the World's Industrial and Cotton Centennial Exposition of New Orleans

ISBN/EAN: 9783337273224

Printed in Europe, USA, Canada, Australia, Japan

Cover: Foto ©Suzi / pixelio.de

More available books at **www.hansebooks.com**

THE EMPIRE OF BRAZIL

AT THE

World's Industrial and Cotton Centennial Exposition,

OF NEW ORLEANS.

NEW YORK:
E. P. COBY & CO., Printers and Stationers,
93 & 95 WILLIAM STREET,
1885.

INDEX.

PAGE.

EXHIBIT OF COFFEE OF BRAZIL AT NEW ORLEANS.—Remarks of the Brazilian
Commission.. 5
A) Table of Production and Consumption of Coffee... 9
B) Table of Last Crops of Brazilian Coffee.. 10
C) Table of Exports of Coffee from Brazil in 1884... 11
D) Statistics of the Receipts and Sales of Coffee in the United States during the last eight years, and
Operations in Brazilian Coffee during the last two years.............................. 12
E) Imports of Coffee into the United States from 1790 to 1819............................... 13
F) Imports of Coffee into the United States from 1821 to 1834.............................. 14
G) Imports of Coffee into the United States by Customs Districts from 1856 to 1882.......... 15
H) Bird's-eye view of the Mississippi River.. 16
THE EMPIRE OF BRAZIL.—Extracts from a paper written by Councillor José Maria da Silva Pa-
ranhos.
    I.—Historical sketch.—Imperial Family.—Political organization.—Religion, Geographical data : Sit-
uation, Surface, Climate, Physical aspects, Mountains, Rivers, Lakes, Harbors, Natural wealth. 19
    II.—Population.—Immigration.—Civilization of the Indians.—Public Instruction.—Scientific Estab-
lishments.—Libraries.—Literary, Scientific, Industrial and Agricultural Societies.—The Press.
    —Charitable and Correctional Institutions.. 22
    III.—Finances.—Army and Navy.—Arsenals.—Military Colonies.—Post Offices and Routes.—Tele-
graphs.—Telephones.—Street Railways.—Railroads.—Highways.—Canals.—Navigation Companies.—Docks.—Light Houses.. 25
    IV.—Commerce.—Proportion of the commerce of Brazil with the other nations.—Principal articles
of export and import.—Table of Brazilian exportation.—Commercial movement of the port of
Rio de Janeiro.—Industry—Agriculture.. 29
COFFEE.—Extract from a Monograph written by Mr. de Sant' Anna Nery.
    I.—General Considerations.. 37
    II.—Coffee from an Economic Standpoint.. 41
A DISCOURSE ON BRAZILIAN COFFEE.—Based upon Analyses made by Prof. Ernst Ludwig
in Vienna, pronounced by Doctor C. Teixeira.
    I.—Liebig's opinion.—Coffee as an excitant of cerebral activity.—Discovery of caffeine.—Coffee as
a source of nutrition : Marvaud's opinion.—Experiments of Stuhlmann, Falck and Leven.—
Opinion of Schultz.—Gasparin.—Effects of coffee upon the bodily exchanges of matter : experiments of Böcker, Lehmann and Marvaud.—Color of the coffee bean : its size, weight and
age.. 47
    II.—History of coffee culture.—Introduction of coffee in Europe.—Coffee in America.—Brazil pro-
duces half of the coffee of the world.—Increase of this production.—Prof. Ernst Ludwig's
analysis of Brazilian coffee.—Brazilian coffee contains more nutritious properties than other
coffees.—Aubert's and Payen's studies.—Table of weight of different coffees shows that Brazilian coffee ranks with the best.. 49
    III.—Why Brazilian coffee is little known in Europe as such.—Foreign denominations given to it,
and only the inferior sorts sold as Brazilian.—Admixtures.—Work of the Association Centro
da Lavoura e Commercio of Rio de Janeiro.—Its exhibitions.—Prices....................... 52
    IV.—The abuse of alcoholic beverages.—Alcoholism checked by the use of coffee.—Great benefit
to nations.—Consumption of coffee per capita for the year 1879.—Conclusion............... 52
BRAZILIAN COFFEE.—Opinions of Scientists on its Merit.................................... 59
EXHIBIT OF COFFEE OF BRAZIL AT NEW ORLEANS.—List of Exhibitors of coffee
from Brazil at the World's Industrial and Cotton Centennial Exposition.................... 67

EXHIBIT OF COFFEE OF BRAZIL

AT THE

WORLD'S INDUSTRIAL AND COTTON CENTENNIAL EXPOSITION

OF NEW ORLEANS,

MADE BY THE ASSOCIATION

Centro da Lavoura e Commercio of Rio de Janeiro,

UNDER THE AUSPICES OF THE

IMPERIAL GOVERNMENT OF BRAZIL.

PRESIDENT OF THE COUNCIL OF MINISTERS AND MINISTER OF FINANCE. *His Excellency Councillor of State, Manoel Pinto de Souza Dantas,* Senator of the Empire.

MINISTER OF THE EMPIRE, PUBLIC INSTRUCTION AND WORSHIP.—*His Excellency Councillor Filippe Franco de Sá,* Senator of the Empire.

MINISTER OF JUSTICE.—*His Excellency Councillor Francisco Maria Sodré Pereira,* Member of the House of Representatives.

MINISTER OF FOREIGN AFFAIRS.—*His Excellency Councillor João da Matta Machado,* Member of the House of Representatives.

MINISTER OF THE NAVY.—*His Excellency Councillor of State Admiral Joaquim Raymundo de Lamare,* Senator of the Empire.

MINISTER OF WAR.—*His Excellency Councillor Candido Luiz Maria de Oliveira,* Member of the House of Representatives.

MINISTER OF AGRICULTURE, COMMERCE AND PUBLIC WORKS.—*His Excellency Councillor Antonio Carneiro da Rocha,* Member of the House of Representatives.

———————

CHIEF OF THE CENTRAL DIRECTORY OF THE DEPARTMENT OF AGRICULTURE, COMMERCE AND PUBLIC WORKS.—*His Excellency Dr. Francisco Leopoldino de Gusmão Lobo,* Ex-Member of the House of Representatives.

COUNCIL OF ADMINISTRATION OF THE ASSOCIATION "CENTRO DA LAVOURA E COMMERCIO."

PRESIDENT.—*His Excellency Viscount de S. Clemente.*

VICE-PRESIDENT.—*Mr. J. C. Ramalho Ortigão.*

SECRETARIES.—*Mr. Honorio Augusto Ribeiro* and *Mr. Hermano Joppert.*

TREASURER.—*His Excellency Baron de Quartin.*

DIRECTORS.—*His Excellency Baron de Araujo Ferraz, Mr. C. A. de Miranda Jordão, Mr. J. de Mello Franco, His Excellency Baron de Araujo Maia, Mr. Bruno Ribeiro* and *Mr. Valverde de Miranda.*

IMPERIAL LEGATION IN WASHINGTON.

CHARGÉ D'AFFAIRES.—*His Excellency José Guryel do Amaral Valente.*

ATTACHES.—*Mr. José Coelho Gomes* and *Mr. Justo Chermont.*

BRAZILIAN COMMISSION AT THE NEW ORLEANS EXPOSITION.

IMPERIAL COMMISSIONER.—*Salvador de Mendonça*, Brazilian Consul General in the United States.

MEMBERS.—*Mr. Allain Eustis*, Vice-Consul of Brazil in New Orleans, and *Mr. G. O. Gordon*, Commissioners of the "Centro da Lavoura e Commercio."

EXHIBIT OF COFFEE OF BRAZIL

AT NEW ORLEANS.

Brazilian coffee, though representing more than one half of the world's production, has been and still continues to be consumed under other names; and the result is, that this article which furnishes the very best qualities to the world's consumption, under the names of Java, Moka, Laguayra, etc., appears in the retail trade under its own name, only in the inferior qualities.

The very great variety of Brazilian coffees has facilitated this fraud, and made it easy to sell the mild and large grained coffees of S. Paulo as Asiatic varieties and the washed coffees of Rio de Janeiro as those of Venezuela, Costa Rica, Martinique or Guatemala.

The only means of restoring the credit of this, Brazil's chief agricultural product, is to show not only the proportion of the production of those countries which compete with it in this country and Europe, rather by brand than by quantity or quality, while on its part it competes with the article and loses the brands, since it becomes, so to speak, denationalized in passing from the importer to the retailer; and to set before the consumer the whole list of its fine varieties, thus bringing together producer and consumer, and furnishing every one with the means of forming his own judgment in the matter, so that the fraud may at least be recognized, if not avoided.

Acquainted with these facts and desirous of remedying the evil, with the purpose of extending the consumption of Brazilian coffees, a new and strong association, composed of representatives of the planters and coffee merchants in the most important port of export of this article, the Centro da Lavoura e Commercio of Rio de Janeiro, acting on a suggestion of Councillor Buarque de Macedo, then Minister of Agriculture, Commerce and Public Works of Brazil, decided in 1881 to hold annual expositions, national and international, of the coffee of Brazil.

In accordance with this plan, expositions of coffee were held in Rio de Janeiro in 1881, 1882, 1883 and 1884, in which the coffees of foreign countries have appeared side by side with those of thousands of native producers, so that these latter could compare their own with foreign products and adopt any improvement recommended by experience. Since the beginning of 1882 up to the present time, the Association has held expositions under the auspices of the Imperial Government in the United States and Europe, under the direction of the consular authorities and delegates at the following places : in the United States, at New York, Boston, and now at New Orleans ; at Montreal, Quebec and Toronto, Canada ; London ; Paris, Nice, Agen and Villeneuve-sur-Lot in France ; Geneva, Lausanne and Zurich, Switzerland ; Amsterdam, Holland ; Berlin, Germany ; Copenhagen, Denmark ; Vienna and Trieste, Austria ; Athens, Greece ; and St. Petersburg, Russia.

Wherever Brazilian coffee has entered into international competition, it has secured the highest premiums. At the Universal Exposition in Paris in 1867 and 1879, at Vienna in 1873, at Philadelphia in 1876, and Buenos Ayres in 1882, it received many premiums. The international jury at Paris in 1867, conferred a gold medal on the coffee of Brazil, a distinction received by no other coffee.

Of the expositions held by the Centro da Lavoura e Commercio in foreign countries, since 1882, those in New York and London received flattering notices from the press of these cities. That at New York, held under the auspices of the New York Coffee Exchange, saw its samples, graded by the Exchange, classed, in some cases, above or equal to the best coffees of the world. At the Berlin Exposition, in 1882, held under the patronage of the Central Society of Commercial Geography of Berlin, the Centro da Lavoura e Commercio and a planter of the Province of S. Paulo obtained the highest prize, the grand diploma of honor ; seven grand diplomas, nine diplomas, and five honorable mentions were given to exhibitors of Brazilian coffees. At the Exposition of coffee at Paris, the grand gold medal of the *Concours Agricole Annuel* was given on the 16th of February, 1883, to the Centro da Lavoura e Commercio. In the same year, at the International Exposition at Amsterdam, the great depot of Dutch coffees, so highly esteemed in Europe, the Centro da Lavoura e Commercio obtained a grand diploma of honor for its exposition of coffees, a premium given to the coffee of no other country. Besides this grand diploma, the jury granted six gold, eleven silver, and fifteen bronze medals, and fifteen honorable mentions to Brazilian planters, and the Dutch Government sent a Commissioner, Mr. van Delden, to Brazil to study the coffee culture of that country.

The purpose of the Association Centro da Lavoura e Commercio of Rio de Janeiro, at the World's Industrial and Cotton Centennial Exposition of New Orleans, in making its exhibit there under the auspices of the Imperial Government, is to prove the excellence of Brazilian coffees in the city which is the natural port of the immense Valley of the Mississippi, where Brazil coffee finds its chief consumption, and which, consequently, should be the natural port of distribution of the article for this zone of its consumption.

The table *A*, appended to these remarks, compiled by Messrs. W. Schöffer & Co., of Rotterdam, shows that the production of coffee, in the past year, for all the world, was 681,314 tons, of which Brazil produced 371,429, and all other countries 309,885 tons ; so that it appears that in 1884 Brazil produced 61,544 tons more than all the other countries together.

The same table shows that, while in the non-producing countries the consumption of coffee in the past year was 734,571 tons, the total production of the world was 681,314 tons, showing an excess of consumption of 53,257 tons over production ; a fact which alone is a sufficient answer to the statement that the decline in the price of coffee is due to excess of production over consumption.

The truth is, that the fall in prices, due principally to the greater facilities for transportation, such as the general substitution of steamers for sailing vessels throughout the world, and the increase of railroad construction in Brazil, which accelerates the delivery of the crops and causes rapid accumulation of stocks, is likewise partly attributable to other causes less easily explained, but related to those pointed out. The lower prices have enlarged the area of consumption, and are preparing the way for a rise in prices, unless production should increase considerably and the supply, during the next few years, be proportional to the demand.

In the tables *B* and *C*, taken from the excellent Commercial Retrospect of the *Jornal do Commercio*, of Rio de Janeiro, of January 9, 1885, are included not only the coffee crops of Brazil exported during the last twenty-five years, but the details of the exportation of 1884, comprising all exporting houses as well as the ports of importation. In connection with the data furnished by these tables, those given in tables *D*, *E*, *F* and *G*, taken from North American sources, will afford the reader interested in this subject a complete body of information, for the study of the condition of the principal product of Brazil, in its largest market, the United States.

At present Brazil need not fear the competition of any country whatever. The superiority of its soil, where the average production for each plant is about six pounds,—three times as much as in Asia and the Dutch possessions, and almost twenty-four times the production per plant in Mexico,—the constant improvements in the culture of coffee in Brazil, which will, in a short time, be perfected in the system of central factories for its treatment and seasoning ; the united efforts of the Imperial Government, and the patriotic Association Centro da Lavoura e Commercio, and of the producers in general, to establish the credit of this product in foreign countries through repeated expositions ; the lowering of the export tax and of freight tariffs on the Brazilian railroads—all these concur to establish the position of Brazil as the foremost coffee-producer of the world. Such is its position in the world's markets that, with the present consumption, should its coffee crop for a single year be destroyed by some catastrophe, prices would rise 110% above the present ones. Of the 252,940 tons sold in the United States in the past year, 168,767 came from Brazil, more than three-fourths of the whole. So vast, though, is the area now devoted to the cultivation of coffee in Brazil that a failure in the supply of this article of prime necessity is altogether improbable.

Now, it is in the export marts of any product that the consumer finds the best supply facilities, because they are not subject to the continual vicissitudes and frequent failures due to a limited cultivation, as is the case in those markets where the entries are small and irregular.

A study of the statistics of production of the world for the last ten years will be sufficient for a recognition of the fact that, as production everywhere, with few exceptions, has diminished, whether from local causes or because of the decline in prices, which in some countries appear to have fallen below the limit of profitable cultivation, in Brazil the advantages already mentioned have maintained a constant increase in production.

It is under circumstances like the present, when the limit of decline in prices appears to have been reached, that the means should be sought for relieving this product from every expense which may be avoided, to the advantage both of producer and consumer.

This is the object of these observations in connection with the Brazilian exposition of coffee at New Orleans.

The Empire of Brazil does not profess a policy of protection ; nevertheless, in consideration of the question of freights on coffee for the United States, it saw that the establishment of a line of steamers under the American flag, in competition with the English steamers, would produce a reduction in freight rates, and therefore determined to grant a subsidy to a new line. The result justified the expectations of the Government, and the rate of freights which eight years ago was 0.75 to $1.00 per bag of coffee, by the English steamers, has fallen to an average of 0.40, and some cargoes have been brought us low as 10 and 15 cents ; so that it has been said of such cargoes that it actually cost less to bring them from Rio de Janeiro to New York, than to transport them, after their arrival, from Brooklyn to the railroads in New York or Jersey City. The truth is that the expense of the subsidy has been a profitable one to Brazil, since it brought about so marked a difference in the freight rates, a difference which more than balances the tax laid to pay the subsidy.

With respect to the Southern ports of the United States, and particularly that of New Orleans, the same benefit has not been fully realized, for the reason that for that port there are no American steamers to compete with the English steamers, and this lack of competition becomes all the more sensible since transportation by steam has almost completely replaced that by sail. It is to be desired that some American or Brazilian line of steamers should supply this want within a short time.

Another circumstance which works to the disadvantage of New Orleans, with respect to the direct importation of coffee from Brazil, is the unnecessary strictness of the quarantine against vessels from Rio de Janeiro and Santos.

Properly viewed, this question can be settled by a single consideration : the fact that the seasons in the two hemispheres are the inverse of each other is sufficient to protect either from any invasion of epidemic from the other. When it is summer in the United States it is winter in Brazil, and *vice versa ;* so that the two countries find a mutual protection in the laws of nature. A few hours of supervision, on both parts, in times of epidemic will be sufficient to guard against infection, the voyages requiring twenty days at least. This subject is worthy of the earnest attention of the United States authorities, who have control of the sanitary regulations of the Southern ports.

The natural consequences of the civil war, the marvelous growth of the port of New York in the last twenty-five years, the consequent concentration of railroad lines towards the commercial emporium of the Union, the mere fact of the triangular commerce between the United States and Brazil, whose products are paid for in London, with the cereals of the former country shipped from New York,—all this has tended to turn from its natural channel the coffee sent from Brazil to the United States.

One who studies the statistics (table *G*) will see that, since the complete interruption in 1862 of the importation of coffee into New Orleans, although there are indications of increase from year to year, the importation has never reached the figures of 1856 to 1860, which exceeded four, five and six million dollars annually, almost equaling, at that time, the importation of New York.

If it is logical that, wherever moves the product of one country, intended to be exchanged for that of another, to this same point the latter should move, it is also natural that the center of consumption of this latter product should seek to re-establish the former channels of supply, as long as said center of consumption remains unchanged.

The United States is at present importing almost two-thirds of the entire production of Brazilian coffee, (see table *C*). Now, the New England States prefer the mild coffees of Asiatic growth, and in default of these, the Brazilian varieties sold by the retail trade as coffees of Asia and the Dutch possessions. The people of the West and North-West, generally, have the same preference, a result, perhaps, of European immigration during the latter half of the present century. It is only in the South, South-West and the central States, that the greater part of the strong-flavored Brazilian coffee is preferred, as is proved by its selling in this zone under its proper name.

Up to the present time, Holland, with a *per capita* consumption of 17.90 pounds, is considered as the greatest coffee-consuming country of the world ; and the United States comes fourth, with a consumption of 8.27 pounds per head, next to Belgium with 9.13 and Norway with 8.73. Taking the whole population of the United States into account, Mr. Joseph Nimmo, Jr., the Chief of the Bureau of Statistics, at Washington, rightly places the United States in the fifth place, as having a *per capita* consumption of 7.42 pounds, next to Cape Colony with 7.72. But if, leaving aside the general rate *per capita*, we consider the real quota of consumption of the different groups of States, we shall find that three-fourths of the consumption belong to the country from New Orleans to Chicago, and that the consumption *per capita* is 15 pounds for the inhabitants of that region, which would place it in the second rank, next to Holland with 17.90 and above Brazil with 10 pounds ; which two countries, probably on account of the extensive use of this beverage, are considered as the most temperate in the world.

Nevertheless, these three-fourths of the importation of Brazilian coffee, turned away from the course of the great river which is its most natural means of transportation, as well as the cheapest, for that whole region, arrive almost entirely at the place of consumption, by way of Chicago, Cincinnati, St. Louis, Louisville, Memphis, etc., after transportation, for a great part of the way, by rail from New York to the valley of the Mississippi.

Supposing freights from Brazilian ports to New York and New Orleans to be the same, the consumers could then decide whether to continue to pay the excess of cost of transportation by rail over that by river. Any one can compare the cost of these different freights, and the result of such comparison is so clear that it is not necessary to enlarge upon it. It is evidently the interest of consumers as well as of producers to rid the article of every expense that can be avoided, since in proportion to the cheapening of the article, the purchasing power of the consumer's money is increased ; and this is almost always followed by increased consumption, in the case of an article of prime necessity.

Economic truths possess the advantage of establishing themselves by their own operations, and do not need the efforts of individual defenders. In the future more or less distant, if the center of consumption of Brazilian coffee remains unchanged, this article will find and follow its route along the course of the Mississippi, almost as naturally as the waters of that river find their way to the Gulf ; but as this is a matter of interest to two enlightened and progressive countries, it seems not too much to expect that the operation of natural law will be anticipated by the enterprise of those who devote themselves to this branch of business. As soon as the great importing houses of New York shall realize the saving that can be made over rates of land transportation, they will doubtless interest themselves more for the supply of the port whence coffee can be most cheaply distributed ; since there is no good reason why cargoes of coffee should not come directly to Southern ports, though Northern houses continue to export the articles which pay for the coffee.

As long as the triangular commerce between the United States and Brazil via Europe shall continue, importers of coffee direct to New Orleans may make cotton take its part with the grains, in the payment, as before the civil war ; and if, as is to be hoped, the commerce of the two countries should be established on its true basis, that of the direct exchange of products, wheat, cotton goods, woolens, silks, machinery, agricultural implements, railroad materials, etc., may be exported from the ports of the South as well as of the North, in exchange for the coffee, rubber, cocoa, sugar, tobacco, wool in the fleece, building woods, etc., of Brazil.

In behalf of the interests of the coffee of Brazil, as well as of the general interests of the commerce of the two countries, the Association Centro da Lavoura e Commercio, of Rio de Janeiro, the Consul General of the Empire, in New York, the Vice-Consul of Brazil, in New Orleans, or in the various other ports of the United States, will be always pleased to furnish any information desired.

In fact the whole business in Brazilian coffee is very well understood in this country ; but the observations above made show that there is something still to be done in order that an article so highly prized by a great part of the population of the Union, may be more cheaply supplied, free from mixtures and frauds, and under its true name, of which the large class of producers, who have devoted themselves to its improvement, have just reason to be proud.

In causing itself to be represented exclusively by this exposition of coffee at New Orleans, and in accord with the views that dictated the selection of the locality for this international exhibition, Brazil has called the attention of the United States to a very important point in the economy of its business relations, destined, no doubt, to become more important, as being to the mutual interest of the two greatest nations of this continent.

A) Production and Consumption of Coffee.

Estimate of last crop of Coffee and its consumption,

As given by the circular of Messrs. W. Schoffer & Co., of Rotterdam, dated August 8, 1884.

PRODUCTION.		CONSUMPTION.	
PRODUCING COUNTRIES.	Tons.	CONSUMING COUNTRIES.	Tons.
Rio de Janeiro (3,250,000 bags)	223,857	United States	245,714
Santos (2,000,000 bags)	137,143	Canada and Pacific	17,143
Bahia and Ceará (167,000 bags)	11,429	Germany	126,457
		France	75,543
Brazil total	371,429	Austria-Hungary	40,914
		Belgium	32,514
Java, Government (piculs) 910,000		Netherlands	28,571
Java, private (do.) 400,000		Sweden, Norway and Denmark	37,143
Sumatra (do.) 100,000		Russia and Poland	11,429
Celebes (do.) 150,000		Switzerland	11,143
		England	16,371
Piculs 1,560,000	109,743	Italy, Spain and Portugal	25,714
		Turkey 14,286	
Venezuela and Central America	101,143	Roumania 11,429	
Porto Rico (less Cuban consumption)	14,857	Levant 8,571	
San Domingo	25,714		
Ceylon	20,571		34,286
English East Indies	20,571	Tunis, Algiers and northern coast of Africa	11,429
Manilla	6,857	Cape of Good Hope, Rio de la Plata and Australia.	20,000
Africa, Moka, etc.	11,429	Total consumption in the non-coffee-producing	
		countries	734,571
Total production of the World	681,314	Total production of the World	681,314
Total production of Brazil	371,424		
		Excess of consumption over production	53,237
Total production of all other countries	309,885		
Excess of production of Brazil over all other countries	61,544		

B) Last Crops of Brazilian Coffee.

Exports of Coffee from Brazil in bags of 60 kilogrammes or 132 pounds each, as given by the Jornal do Commercio of Rio de Janeiro, of January 9, 1885:

Years, ending June 30.	Quantities.	Years, ending December 31.	Countries whither exported.		
			United States.	Europe, and all others.	Total.
	Bags.		Bags.	Bags.	Bags.
1859–1860	2,050,249	1860	1,408,845	1,416,312	2,825,157
1860–1861	3,185,091	1861	907,293	1,626,241	2,533,534
1861–1862	2,310.036	1862	473,300	1,346,266	1,819,656
1862–1863	1,736,928	1863	456,706	1,195,553	1,652,259
1863–1864	1,661,270	1864	671,389	1,140,540	1,811,929
1864–1865	2,209.620	1865	863,000	2,333,504	3,197,464
1865–1866	1,983,360	1866	1,928,743	1,339,892	3,268,635
1866–1867	2,584,978	1867	1,501,606	1,754,374	3,255,980
1867–1868	2,810,798	1868	1,404,120	1,368,800	2,772,920
1868–1869	1,940,334	1869	1,526,374	1,613,415	3,139,789
1869–1870	3,190,243	1870	1,680,269	1,024,473	2,704,742
1870–1871	3,337,985	1871	1,656,844	1,227,782	2,884,626
1871–1872	2,113,113	1872	1,383,193	1,077,158	2,460,351
1872–1873	3,040,062	1873	1,435,800	1,0v7,909	2,483,709
1873–1874	2,007,403	1874	1,521,499	1,151,782	2,673,281
1874–1875	3,205,467	1875	2,041,995	1,110.301	3,152,296
1875–1876	2,889,990	1876	1,448,424	1,317,408	2,765,922
1876–1877	2,781,642	1877	1,710,073	1,136,482	2,846,555
1877–1878	2,632,746	1878	1,670,383	1,360,816	3,031,199
1878–1879	3,705,840	1879	2,283,545	1,251,638	3,535,183
1879–1880	2,990,058	1880	1,896,857	1,676,197	3,563,054
1880–1881	4,401,627	1881	2,241,076	2,135,442	4,377,418
1881–1882	3,926,372	1882	2,459,132	1,741,458	4,200,590
1882–1883	4,556,373	1883	2,314,650	1,339,861	3,654,511
1883–1884	3,138,721	1884	2,401,105	1,496,008	3,897,113

C) Table of Exports of Coffee from Brazil in 1884.

(From the Jornal do Commercio of Rio de Janeiro, of January 9, 1885.)

HOUSES OF EXPORTERS IN THE PORTS OF BRAZIL.

Houses.	Quantities.	Houses.	Quantities.	Houses.	Quantities.
	Bags of 60 kil.		*Bags of 60 kil.*		*Bags of 60 kil.*

PORTS WHITHER EXPORTED.

United States:	*Bags of 60 kil.*	Total.

1) Statistics of the Receipts and Sales of Coffee in the United States during the last 8 years, and operations in Brazilian Coffee during the last 2 years, ending December 31.

As given by the circulars of Messrs. Wm. Scott's Sons, of New York, dated January 1, 188.. and 188..

C(

North
Flo
Brit
All

West
Brit
Dan
Dut
Fra
Spa
Swe
Hay
All

Centr
Coa
Hon

Europ
Eng
Hav
Fra
Hol
Por
Spa
All

Asia :
Chi
Brit
Dut
All

Africa
Cap
Bou
Brit
All

In c
All

E) IMPORTS OF COFFEE.

Statement, by countries, showing the quantity of Coffee imported into the United States each year ended September 30, from 1790 to 1891, both inclusive.

829...
830..
831...
832...
833...
834...
835..
836...
837...
838...
839..
840...
841...
842...
June
843b..
844...
845..
846...
847...
848...
849...
850...
851...
852...
853...
854...
855...
856...
857...
858...
859..
860...
861...

862...

863...
864...
905...
866...
867..
868...
8 i0...
870...

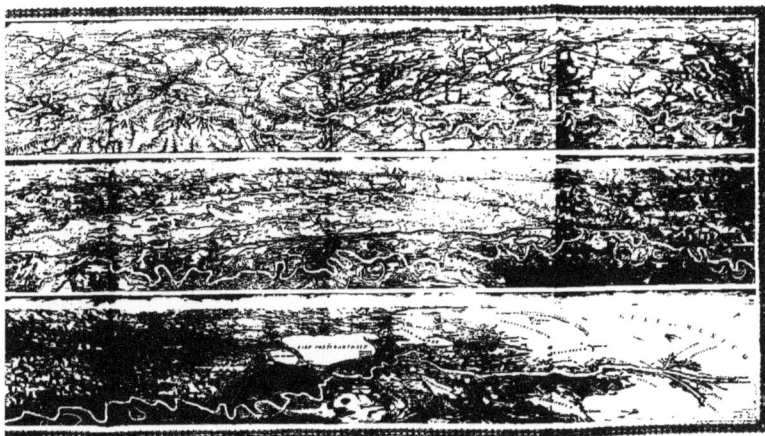

" BIRD'S-EYE VIEW of the MISSISSIPPI RIVER
FROM THE MOUTH OF THE MISSOURI TO THE GULF OF MEXICO.
1881.

THE EMPIRE OF BRAZIL.

EXTRACTS FROM A PAPER

WRITTEN BY

Councillor JOSÉ MARIA DA SILVA PARANHOS,

——◄ Commissioner of the Imperial Government at the ►——

Exposition of St. Petersburg, 1884.

THE EMPIRE OF BRAZIL.

I.

Historical sketch.— Imperial Family.— Political organization.— Religion.— Geographical data: Situation, Surface, Climate, Physical Aspects, Mountains, Rivers, Lakes, Harbors, Natural Wealth.

The Empire of Brazil is a new country : scarcely sixty-two years having elapsed since the declaration of its independence.

Discovered by the Portuguese in 1500, it was only until thirty years later that it was settled. The first settlers had to struggle against the savage and warlike tribes that peopled the country ; and afterwards were obliged to resist invaders from Europe, particularly the Dutch, then at the height of their power, and who, during a part of the XVII century, were successful in maintaining their settlements along the northern coast. After a struggle of about thirty years, all the territory in the hands of the Dutch was reconquered, and the unity of Brazil definitely assured.*

In 1808 the Royal Family of Bragança established itself in Rio de Janeiro, which thus became the capital of the Portuguese monarchy ; and from that time all the ports of Brazil were opened to the commerce of the world, by edict of the Prince Regent, the same who afterwards, under the name of Dom John VI, became King of Portugal.

In 1815 Brazil was raised to the rank of Kingdom, and made part of the "United Kingdom of Portugal, Brazil and Algarves." When, in 1821, the King returned to Portugal, Dom Pedro, heir to the crown, remained in Brazil as Prince Regent.

In 1822, putting himself at the head of the Brazilian people, who aspired to independence, Dom Pedro proclaimed the separation of Brazil, on the 7th of September, in the midst of universal rejoicing. He was proclaimed Emperor October 12, 1822, and took the oath of fidelity to the Constitution.

Dom Pedro I, who had, in 1826, abdicated the crown of Portugal, in 1831 abdicated that of Brazil, and went to Europe to support the rights of his daughter, the Princess Donna Maria.

This chivalrous Prince died in 1834 at the age of thirty six years, leaving on the throne of Portugal his daughter, the Queen Donna Maria, and on that of Brazil his son, His Majesty Dom Pedro II, the present Emperor.

Brazil owes its independence to Dom Pedro I ; and to him also it owes the integrity of its territory and its political institutions.

During the minority of the second Emperor, while the State was governed by a regency, the country passed through a period disturbed by revolutions and outbreaks in several of the provinces.

In 1840, His Majesty Dom Pedro II reached his recognized majority, and from that date order was everywhere re-established, and the Empire entered resolutely in the way of progress under the wise direction of this firm and enlightened Prince.

The Government of Brazil is a monarchy, hereditary, constitutional and representative.

His Majesty Dom Pedro II, son of the founder of the Empire and the Empress Leopoldina, Archduchess of Austria, was born at Rio de Janeiro December 2d, 1825, and succeeded his august father April 7th, 1831. On the 23d of July, 1840, his majority was proclaimed, and he was crowned July 18th of the following year. In 1843 he married Her Majesty Donna Theresa, daughter of Francis I, King of the Two Sicilies.

The heiress to the throne is Her Imperial Highness Donna Isabel, Princess Imperial, married to His Imperial Highness Prince Gaston d'Orleans, Count d'Eu, Marshal of the army of Brazil, eldest son of His Royal Highness the Duke de Nemours.

The children of this marriage are : the Princes Dom Pedro, Prince of Gram-Pará (October 15th, 1875) ; Dom Luiz Maria Phillippe (January 26th, 1878) ; and Dom Antonio Gaston (August 9th, 1881).

From the marriage of the deceased Princess Donna Leopoldina, second daughter of the Emperor, and His Royal Highness Prince Augustus, Duke of Saxe, were born : the Princes Dom Pedro Augusto (March 19th, 1866) ; Dom Augusto (December 6th, 1867) ; Dom José Fernando (May 21st, 1869) ; Dom Luiz Gaston (September 16th, 1870).

The Political Constitution of Brazil dates from March 25th, 1824, and has been in part modified by the Additional Act of 1834. It recognizes four branches of political powers : the legislative, moderative, executive and judiciary.

The Legislative Power is vested in the Chamber of Deputies and the Senate, with the sanction of the Emperor.

The Senate is composed of fifty-eight members, elected for life. Whenever there is a vacancy in the body, the electors of the province to which the seat belongs present to the Emperor for his selection a list of three names.

---

* Thanks to this long colonial period and the struggles that characterized it, the history of Brazil has in record many memorable deeds, and its soil bears the imprints of the passage of the greatest European nations, during the three centuries that precede our own. The fleets of the famous Portuguese discoverers of the lands of Africa and Asia entered its harbors, and in its waters were engaged many great naval conflicts between the armadas of Spain and Holland. Bahia, S. Paulo and Rio de Janeiro possess temples, monasteries and aqueducts as worthy of notice as the analogous monuments of the Latin countries of Europe. Pernambuco retains more relics of the Dutch occupation than New York, and of the administration of Prince John Maurice of Nassau, who in 1637, scarcely seventeen years after the arrival of the Pilgrims in New England, and ten years before the Rhode Island declaration of religious freedom, had already proclaimed in Recife the liberty of conscience.

For the election of Deputies, the capital of the Empire and the provinces are divided into electoral districts, since the reform of January 9th, 1881, which established direct suffrage. Each district chooses a deputy. The Chamber is elected for four years and may be dissolved by the Emperor.

The Emperor is chief of the Executive Power, and governs through his Ministers of State.

There are seven ministerial departments : Ministry of Finance ; of the Empire (Interior, Public Instruction, Worship) ; of Justice ; of Foreign Affairs ; of War ; of the Marine, and of Agriculture, Commerce and Public Works. The President of the Council takes one of the ministerial departments.

The Council of State is composed of twenty-four members ; and although it is purely consultative, it is a most important aid towards assuring good administration. The heir or heiress of the throne is a member of this Council ; but the other princes of the imperial family, and the husband of the heiress presumptive to the throne, only take part in it when called upon by the Emperor.

The Judiciary is independent, and the judges hold for life. In the more important provinces there are courts of appeal and courts of commerce. The supreme tribunal of justice sits at Rio de Janeiro.

The Moderative Power is delegated exclusively to the Emperor as supreme chief of the nation, that he may constantly guard the maintenance of independence, the balance and harmony of the other branches of the political powers.

The twenty provinces of the Empire are governed by presidents appointed by the Imperial Government. Each province has a Legislative Assembly chosen by popular vote ; and in each city is a municipal chamber.

The State religion is the Roman Catholic, which is also the religion of nearly all the Brazilians ; but all others are tolerated, and no one can be disturbed on account of his religious opinions.

The Empire of Brazil occupies the eastern part of South America, and its boundaries touch every other country of this part of the New World, except Chili. It is comprised between latitudes 5° 10′ North and 33° 46′ 10″ South, and longitudes 8° 21′ 24″ East and 32° West, from the meridian of Rio de Janeiro.*

This vast Empire comprises one-fifteenth part of the land surface of the globe, one-fifth of the two Americas, or more than three-sevenths of South America.

Its surface contains 8,337,218 square kilometres, or sixteen times the extent of France or Germany, and thirty times that of Italy. In extent of territory Brazil comes next to the Russian Empire, the British Empire and China.

The soil of Brazil is very broken, especially in the central and northern parts. Broad plateaus and vast plains extend into the interior ; and mighty rivers, in great part navigable, water and fertilize the land.

The climate is hot and moist in the intra-tropical belt during the rainy season ; elsewhere it is temperate and relatively dry. In the valley of the Amazon, under the equator, the mean temperature is 27° Centigrade, but the elevation of the surface, the vegetation and the East winds, modify greatly the effects of the heat. Even close to the equator, districts may be found where the climate is mild in summer and cold in winter. From Pará to the Province of S. Paulo the climate along the coast is quite hot ; but leaving the coast, the temperature sensibly diminishes, under the influence of the mountain chains that follow the coast line, and of the elevation of the surface. Thus, at Rio de Janeiro it is very hot during the summer, but at a short distance from that city, in the suburbs situated on the surrounding heights, one may enjoy a delightful climate, temperate all the year round.

The Provinces of Minas Geraes, Paraná, Santa Catharina, Rio Grande do Sul and S. Paulo, with the exception of the coast of this latter, present a climate similar to that of Southern Europe.

Outside of the low and marshy lands and the banks of certain water-courses, where, at certain seasons of the year, intermittent fevers prevail, one does not find in Brazil those severe maladies which are wont to decimate great populations. Such was the opinion of the author of "The Climate and Maladies of Brazil." He considered that country, which he had visited and where he had long lived, as one of the most healthful of the globe ; and he added that Brazil is to the New World what Italy is to the Old.

In Europe, whenever Brazil is mentioned, one thinks of the yellow fever. This is due to the exaggerations of certain travelers. The yellow fever made its first appearance in Rio de Janeiro in 1850, and since that date, it is met with from time to time in the great cities of the seaboard, but never penetrates into the interior. It is true that at Rio, as at Santos, Bahia and Pernambuco, there is always, during the summer, a certain number of cases of yellow fever ; but, all other things being equal, this disease slays no more in our maritime cities than typhoid fever in Paris. It is particularly those newly arrived in the country who are attacked by this disease, unless they take certain hygienic precautions, indispensable on a change of climate. The Government does not permit during the warm season the collection of great numbers of immigrants in the maritime cities. As fast as they arrive new immigrants are sent into the interior and to the colonies to which they are destined.

The orographic system of Brazil is composed of four great chains : in the centre the Serra do Espinhaço, or Serra da Mantiqueira ; at the East the Serra do Mar, which follows the coast for a great distance ; at the West the Serra das Vertentes, and at the North, beyond the Amazon, the Serras de Pacarayma, Acaray and Tumucuraque.

The central chain, from its elevation and numerous spurs, is the most important. The peak of Itatiaia, which belongs to this chain, is the highest point in Brazil, being about 3,000 metres high.

Brazil is watered by four great streams : the Amazon, Tocantins, Paraná and S. Francisco.

The Amazon, rising in Peru, has a length of 3,828 kilometres on Brazilian soil, and receives the waters of many affluents, some of which are more than 3,300 kilometres in length. The Tocantins, and its principal affluent, the Araguaya, have each a length of more than 2,600 kilometres.

The Amazon and Tocantins, with their branches, serve as the means of communication between the Provinces of Pará, Amazonas and Goyaz, part of the Provinces of Maranhão and Matto Grosso, and the Republics of Venezuela, Colombia, Equador, Peru and Bolivia. The Amazon and its tributaries offer, on Brazilian territory alone, a length of 43,250 kilometres navigable for steamboats. Several steam navigation companies, subsidized by the General Government or by the Provinces of Amazonas and Pará, are engaged in the navigation of the Tocantins and Araguaya. English steamships from Liverpool ply between England and the chief cities of the two provinces,† and another regular line of French steamers has been inaugurated, during the past year, between Havre and Pará, which is the principal outlet for the productions of the rich valley of the Amazon.

The Paraná, formed by the confluence of the Rio Grande and the Paranahyba, crosses the Brazilian Provinces of S. Paulo, Matto Grosso and Paraná, and the Argentine Provinces of Misiones, Corrientes, Entre-Rios and Santa Fé.

---

* The meridian of Rio de Janeiro is 43° 7′ 6″ West from Greenwich.

† Another line of English steamships is running between these same places and the City of New York.

Of its tributaries, the Paraguay is the most considerable, and itself has branches also navigable. The communication between Matto Grosso and the capital of the Empire is made by steamboats, along the Paraguay, the Paraná and the La Plata.

The S. Francisco crosses the Province of Minas Geraes, in which it rises, and those of Bahia, Pernambuco, Alagôas and Sergipe. Navigation is interrupted by the falls of Paulo Affonso, but a railroad has been built to connect the two navigable portions of the river, towards which the great railroad lines of Rio de Janeiro, Bahia and Pernambuco are directed.

Besides the rivers belonging to the four great basins just mentioned, several others of considerable importance empty into the Atlantic ; among which may be mentioned the Gurupy, Tury Assú, Itapicurú, Parnahyba, Jaguaribe, Piranhas, Parahyba, Vasa-Barris, Paraguassú, Rio de Contas, Jequitinhonha, Mucury, Rio Doce and Parahyba do Sul. The basin of the lakes dos Patos and Mirim, in the Province of Rio Grande do Sul, is traversed by several great rivers which empty into these lakes, as the Jacuhy, the Camaquan and the Jaguarão.

Another great river, the Uruguay, which rises in the Province of Santa Catharina, serves as the boundary between the Province of Rio Grande do Sul and the Argentine Republic, and forms, further on, with the Paraná, the vast estuary of the La Plata.

Along the Atlantic coast, which has an extent of 7,920 kilometres, communication is made by numerous Brazilian or foreign steamship lines. All the provinces, except those of Minas Geraes, Goyaz, Amazonas and Matto Grosso, touch the Atlantic and have harbors. The four interior provinces have communication with the sea through the great waterways already named ; and that of Minas Geraes is already in connection with the coast by railroads.

The principal ports are those of Belem do Pará, S. Luiz de Maranhão, Parnahyba, Recife de Pernambuco, Maceió, Bahia, Victoria, Rio de Janeiro, Santos, Paranaguá, Santa Catharina and Rio Grande do Sul. The harbor or port of Rio de Janeiro has a circuit of more than 198 kilometres.

In Brazil are found diamonds, emeralds, sapphires, rubies, topazes, beryls, garnets and cornalines, black, blue and green, known by the name of Brazilian emeralds. There are exported considerable blocks of rock crystal of great purity, as well as amethysts, opals, agates, jasper and veined crystal of yellow quartz. Gold abounds in Brazil, and several mines are worked at the present time ; the richest being in the Province of Minas Geraes. There are also found silver, copper, iron, antimony, mercury, tin, zinc, lead, bismuth and arsenic.

Brazil furnishes granites of various colors, and marbles, the most remarkable of which are the green and black marbles of Rio Grande do Sul. The vast coast region between latitudes 15° and 30° South is composed almost entirely of primitive rocks, such as granites, gneiss, diorites, green and black, light and dark quartzites, porphyries and syenites. In the interior are found ferruginous rocks, sandstones, pure or ferruginous, and limestones suitable for sculpture, and susceptible of being polished like marble. The lime that is used in building along the coast is made almost exclusively of oyster shells. Fibrous plaster is found in the Province of Minas and in several of the northern ones. Several varieties of clays, white or pink, are used in the manufacture of crockery, tiles, crucibles and common ware. Kaolin, which abounds in Brazil, is almost always mixed with quartz.

Coal is found in several provinces, especially in those of Rio Grande do Sul, Santa Catharina and Paraná. The coal beds of Candiota and Arroio dos Ratos, in the first of these provinces, and that of Tubarão in Santa Catharina, are being worked, and railroads have been constructed to facilitate the transportation. Deposits of lignite, peat, bituminous schists, graphite and sulphur are abundant.

Among the salts most abundant may be mentioned saltpetre, alum, rock salt, chloride of sodium or common salt, and the sulphates of magnesium and sodium. Important beds of phosphate of lime have been recently discovered on three islands of Fernando de Noronha group, and their productive capacity has been estimated at 1,300,000 metric tons.

Mineral springs are numerous ; among them iron, alkaline, saline, sulphurous ; and besides these there are hot springs.

Of alimentary plants, the most important are coffee, sugar-cane, mate or Paraguay tea, Indian corn, rice, wheat and rye. Among the fruits we will mention only the pine-apple, banana, cocoa plant, mango, chestnut, plum, fig, goyaba and orange, also the peach and the pear. The great variety of situations and climate of the different parts of Brazil adapt it to the culture of almost all the plants in the world. To give an idea of the amazing fertility of the soil, it is enough to mention that Indian corn yields an average of 200 for 1, and on selected lands, of 400 for 1 ; and that rice, which grows abundantly on the well watered plains, produces as much as 1,000 for 1.

The textile plants are flax, the piassabas (*Attalea funifera* and *Leopoldinia Piassava*), the tucum (*Bactris Lelosa* and *Astrocaryum tucuman*), the Indian cocoa (*Cocus nucifera*), the *Acrocomia sclerocarpa*, the *Lecythis speciosa*, the *Platonia insignis*, the *Fourcroya gigantea*, the *Agave Americana*, and *Agave Mexicana*, the *Urena lobata*, and a very great number of other plants, from which may be made from the coarsest cordage to tissues the very finest. Cotton is cultivated in all the northern and some of the central provinces.

Several sorts of oil-producing plants, not known in Europe, are found. The exportation of gum copal, of India-rubber and resins is one of the chief sources of wealth. The rubber trade alone gives to the Government a revenue of about $1,400,000 annually.

Brazil produces nutmegs, vanilla, cloves, cinnamon and many other aromatic plants.

Among the finest varieties of woods suitable for carpenter or joiner work, cabinet-making and naval construction, we will mention only the iron wood, the Brazilian yellow wood, satin wood, red and white cedar and rosewood of various shades.

Among the useful vegetables, the carnauba, (*Copernicia cerifera*), which so largely supplies the industrial and alimentary needs of man, deserves a special mention. It grows without cultivation in the northern provinces.

The ox, the sheep and horse multiply almost without the care of man. The number of heads of cattle is estimated at more than 30,000,000. representing a capital of at least $85,000,000.

The deer, wild boar, armadillo, agouti, tapir, paca, otter and many other useful animals abound.

In Brazil are found the most beautiful and varied species of birds, of which we will name only the Brazilian pelican, the cyenas nigricolis, snipe, ema, partridge, quail, pigeon, parrot and ara.

The reptiles are likewise numerous, the most remarkable of which are the rattle-snake, the boa, the chameleon, alligator, and lastly, the tortoise, whose flesh is excellent, and supplies what is called tortoise butter, in the Province of the Amazonas.

The varieties of fishes are innumerable. Prof. Agassiz alone collected thousands in the valley of the Amazon. One sort, the Pirarucú, forms the principal food of the inhabitants of the Provinces of Pará and Amazonas.

II.

Population.—Immigration.—Civilization of the Indians.—Public Instruction.—Scientific Establishments.—Libraries.—Literary, Scientific, Industrial and Agricultural Societies.—The Press.—Charitable and Correctional Institutions.

The population of Brazil, to-day, is only 12,000,000; a very small number, it is true, for so vast a territory, but which is rapidly increasing; in the first place from births, and secondly, and still more, from European immigration. This country, with its truly wonderful riches and natural fertility, where existence is so easy, might easily support 700,000,000 inhabitants, if the population were as dense as that of Germany, France and other countries of Europe. The inhabitants belong in part to the Caucasian, African and Indian races, and partly to crosses between these races, in the following proportions :

Of pure Caucasian race..............................One-third.
Of African or Indian................................One-third.
Of Metis or mixed ....One-third.

The foreigners number about 300,000, of whom more than one-half are Portuguese ; the Germans and Italians coming next.

The following table gives the capital, area and population of each Province :

MUNICIPALITY OF THE CAPITAL OF THE EMPIRE AND PROVINCES.	CHIEF CITIES.	AREA, SQUARE KILOMETRES.	POPULATION.		TOTAL.
			FREE.	SLAVE.*	
Municipality...............	Rio de Janeiro......	1,394	400,000	35,568 (1879)	435,568
Provinces:					
Amazonas.........	Manáos	1,897,020	80,000	942 (1879)	80,942
Pará......................	Belem do Pará......	1,149,712	320,000	23,511 (1882)	343,511
Maranhão..................	São Luiz	459,884	370,000	60,059 (1882)	430,059
Piauhy	Theresina	301,797	221,000	18,691 (1882)	239,691
Ceará.....................	Fortaleza...........	104,250	722,000	——— (1884)	722,000
Rio Grande do Norte........	Natal..............	57,485	259,000	10,051 (1882)	269,051
Parahyba..................	Parahyba........	74,731	407,000	25,817 (1882)	432,817
Pernambuco................	Recife..............	128,395	930,000	84,700 (1882)	1,014,700
Alagôas...................	Maceió	58,491	368,000	29,379 (1882)	397,379
Sergipe	Aracajú............	39,090	185,000	26,173 (1882)	211,173
Bahia	Bahia..............	426,427	1,490,000	165,403 (1882)	1,655,403
Espirito Santo..............	Victoria............	44,839	80,000	20,717 (1882)	100,717
Rio de Janeiro.............	Nictheroy..........	68,982	670,000	268,831 (1882)	938,831
S. Paulo..................	S. Paulo	290.876	890,000	168,950 (1876)	1,058,950
Paraná....................	Corityba	221,319	182,000	7,668 (1882)	189,668
Santa Catharina............	Desterro............	74,156	190,000	11,043 (1882)	201,043
Rio Grande do Sul	Porto Alegre.......	236,553	500,000	68,703 (1882)	568,703
Minas Geraes	Ouro Preto.........	574,855	2,170,000	279,010 (1882)	2,449,010
Goyaz....................	Goyaz.............	747,311	185,000	6,711 (1879)	191,711
Matto Grosso	Cuyabá	1,379,651	65,000	7,051 (1876)	72,051
	Totals........	8,337,218 square kilom.	10,654,000	1,318,978 †	12,002,978
Savage Indians............................					600,000
					12,602,978 Inhabitants.

(*) The figures in parenthesis denote the year of the last census at our disposal.

† The slave population at present (1884) is no more (1,318,978). According to the latest statistics, the number of slaves is reduced to 1,150,000, and the free population has considerably increased. In 1873 the number of slaves was 1,540,790, so that in ten years there has been a diminution of 390,000. The two Provinces of Ceará and Amazonas have no longer a slave.

The following is the population of the principal cities :

Rio de Janeiro, capital of the Empire	350,000
Nictheroy, capital of the Province of Rio de Janeiro	30,000
Bahia	140,000
Recife de Pernambuco	130,000
Belem do Pará	40,000
S. Paulo	40,000
S. Luiz do Maranhão	35,000
Porto Alegre	35,000
Ouro Preto	20,000
Rio Grande	18,000
Santos	14,000

In the above table the slaves represent a tenth part of the population. It is unfortunate that Brazil could not, like Russia, accomplish at one stroke a reform like that which will be forever the glory of Alexander II ; but in Brazil the whole agricultural prosperity was based on slave labor. The work of emancipation, however, which could not be accomplished at once without danger is gradually being wrought out, without shock and without injury to the sources of production and to the national prosperity.

The slave trade was abolished in 1851. A law of the 28th of September, 1871,* declared free thenceforth every child born of slave parents, and set apart the revenue from certain taxes for the liberation of the slaves born previously to the passage of the law. Since that epoch the great proprietors and the entire Brazilian nation, supporting the generous efforts of the Imperial Government, have lent their aid to the work of emancipation.

On the 25th of March last, the Province of Ceará freed all the slaves in its territory, and this event was celebrated throughout the Empire with great rejoicings.

The day is in sight, in the not distant future, when none but free men will be found in the Empire of Brazil.

The Imperial Government favors colonization in the most liberal and intelligent manner. State, provincial and individual colonies have been organized to receive new immigrants and put them in the way of gaining a good and certain livelihood.

Every immigrant arriving at Rio de Janeiro finds protection and assistance from the Department of Public Lands and Colonization, whose agents and interpreters board the trans-atlantic steamers. The new colonists are taken to a place of lodging, supported by the Government, where they are lodged and fed, and where they receive information to enable them to make a selection of lands for settlement according to their aptitude and taste. They are then transported to the colony of their selection, where they find lands purchasable at the lowest price, and are given easy means for supplying themselves with implements of labor.†

The paternal and enlightened care of the Government for immigrants has borne good fruits, and a current of immigration from Europe to Brazil, which is every day increasing, has been established. This movement is entirely spontaneous, under the influence of the good results attained by the colonists already settled in Brazil upon their families and friends remaining in Europe.

For some years Brazil has had no agencies, as have other South American States, in foreign lands, for the purpose of soliciting immigration. The arrivals of immigrants in the ports of Rio de Janeiro alone has been as follows : in 1870, 9,123 ; in 1871, 12,331 ; in 1872, 18,441 ; in 1873, 14,931 ; in 1877, 29,027 ; in 1878, 22,423 ; in 1880, 22,859 ; in 1882, 25,845. Last year the number landed at Rio de Janeiro was 30,000. As Brazil has several large ports having direct connections with Europe, it is probably no exaggeration to place the average annual immigration at present at 40,000.

Among the 25,845 immigrants landed at Rio in 1882 were 10,562 Italians, principally Tyroleans and Lombards, 9,269 Portuguese, 3,738 Spaniards, 1,569 Germans, 249 Frenchmen, 239 Englishmen, and 219 of other nationalities, of whom only 19 were Russians.

A "Central Immigration Society" has been recently established at Rio de Janeiro, under the presidency of Count Henrique de Beaurepaire Rohan, general of the Brazilian army, formerly Minister of War, and the vice-presidency of Major A. d'Escragnolle Taunay, member of the Chamber of Deputies, both belonging to Brazilian families of French extraction. This society renders valuable assistance to the Department of Public Lands and Colonization, and occupies itself with all questions concerning the welfare and protection of the colonists and the development of colonization.

Colonies at first established under the protection of the State or of the provinces have soon become prosperous and strong enough no longer to require that assistance. Among these are several cities classed among the most prosperous. We may mention among these S. Leopoldo, in the Province of Rio Grande do Sul, whose district contains more than 60,000 inhabitants of German origin ; the ancient colonies of Blumenau and Donna Francisca, in the Province of Santa Catharina, within which have sprung up the towns of Annabourg and Joinville ; and Petropolis and Nova Friburgo, in the Province of Rio de Janeiro, summer resorts for the wealthy citizens of the capital. During the summer the Imperial Court has its residence at Petropolis.

---

* The passage of this law was due to the late Councillor of State, José Maria da Silva Paranhos, Viscount of Rio Branco, father of the author of this sketch, then President of the Council of Ministers.

† To voluntary immigrants to Brazil the following favors are extended : food and lodging in Rio de Janeiro for eight days at most ; free transportation by the railroads of the Government, or by the lines of steamers subsidized by it, to the place of destination ; and the sale of Government lands, on the following conditions : The price per acre of country tracts will vary from $0.42 to $1.08, and from $2.10 to $16.80 for town lots, according to fertility, situation and other circumstances. Colonists, on their arrival, may choose freely the lands they prefer, by paying cash, at the price fixed, according to classification. For those buying on credit, 20 per cent. will be added to the above prices, and the payment shall be made in five equal installments, counting from the end of the second year of the settlement of the land. Those colonists, however, who shall pay before these respective times of payment, shall have a reduction of 6 per cent. corresponding to the whole amount of the debt, or of the payments made before due.

With respect to the indigenes, who form a population estimated at more than 600,000, the Government has made efforts to civilize them, with the aid of the missionaries, who give them religious and other instructions. Villages have thus been formed, where these Indians, abandoning their former wandering life, devote themselves to agricultural pursuits.

Public instruction is gratuitous. The following figures will give an idea of the number of primary public schools and the number of pupils attending them since 1857.

1857......................	2,595 primary public schools,			70,124 pupils.
1866.......................	4,435 "	"	"	107,483 "
1872......................	4,653 "	"	"	155,058 "
1878......................	5,661 "	"	"	175,714 "
1881......................	5,785 "	"	"	188,843 "

Besides the free primary schools, supported by the governments of the provinces or by the Imperial Government in the municipality of the capital, there are in existence lyceums for higher instruction and numerous private institutions, both for primary instruction and for the studies preparatory to the higher schools.

Among the institutions for higher or professional instruction may be mentioned the Medical Faculties of Rio and Bahia, the Faculties of Law at S. Paulo and Pernambuco, the Polytechnic School, the Military Schools, the Naval School, the School of Mines, the Normal School, the Academy of Fine Arts, the Conservatory of Music, the Commercial Institute, the Lyceum of Arts and Trades, the Seminaries, the Imperial Institute for Blind Youths, the Deaf and Dumb Institute, the Agricultural Institutes, etc.

The principal scientific establishments, museums and libraries are :

At Rio de Janeiro, the Imperial Astronomical Observatory, the National Museum, the National Library, with about 140,000 volumes, the Libraries of the Faculty of Medicine, of the Historical and Geographical Institute, of the Polytechnic School, of the Academy of Fine Arts, of the Military School, of the General Bureau of Statistics, of the Army, of the Navy, the Libraries Fluminense and Municipal, those of the Portuguese Cabinet of Reading, of the Monastery of S. Benedict and of the convents of S. Antonio and the Carmelites, the museums of the Army and of the Navy, and the Pedagogic Museum.

At Pará, Fortaleza, Maceió and Ouro Preto, there are museums worthy of mention ; and all the capitals of the provinces and the principal cities possess libraries of greater or less importance.

The Astronomical Observatory, the National Museum, the National Library and the School of Mines publish Scientific Annals, known and appreciated by the scientists of Europe.

We will mention among the scientific, literary and industrial societies established at Rio de Janeiro, the Historical, Geographic and Ethnographic Institute of Brazil, which hold fortnightly sessions at the Imperial Palace, and whose sittings are always honored by the presence of the Emperor, (its *Review* already forms forty-seven thick volumes) ; the Imperial Academy of Medicine (Annals) : the Brazilian Polytechnic Institute, presided over by His Imperial Highness, the Count d'Eu, (Review) ; the Geographical Society of Rio de Janeiro ; the Institute of the Order of Advocates ; the Brazilian Institute of Physical Sciences ; the Vellosiana Society (Natural Sciences and History of the Aborigines); the Institute of Directors and Professors ; the League of Instruction in Brazil ; the Imperial Society in Aid of Instruction ; the Society in Aid of National Industry (Review) ; the Society for the Propagation of the Fine Arts ; the Society in Aid of the Mechanic and Liberal Arts ; the Brazilian Society of Acclimatization, the Horticultural and Agricultural Association, under the presidency of His Imperial Highness, the Count d'Eu ; the Central Association of Agriculture and Commerce (Centro da Lavoura e Commercio) ; the Central Immigration Society.

In the provinces we may mention the Historical and Geographical Institutes of Bahia and of Rio Grande do Sul, the Archeological Institutes of Pernambuco and of Alagoas, the Society for the Propagation of Public Instruction in Pernambuco, which has established a normal school at Recife.

The press is represented by numerous journals in every part of the Empire and particularly in the capital, the capitals of the provinces and the great cities. Rio de Janeiro possesses more than forty journals, three of which are published in English, two in French, one in German and one in Italian. The most important are the *Diario Official*, the *Jornal do Commercio*, the *Gazeta de Noticias*, the *Gazeta da Tarde*, the *Diario do Brazil*, the *Folha Nova*, and the *Brazil*. Several among them, both as to form and number of pages, will compare favorably with the larger political and commercial journals of England and the United States. The largest Brazilian journals are the *Jornal do Commercio*, at Rio de Janeiro, and the *Diario de Pernambuco*, at Pernambuco. The former of these is 0ᵐ.71 long by 0ᵐ.63 wide, and the number of pages varies from six to sixteen ; the type used is minion. The *Gazeta de Noticias* of Rio has the largest circulation.

Charitable establishments and associations are very numerous in Brazil. Some of the hospitals, particularly the Misericordia and the Dom Pedro II hospital at Rio de Janeiro, are veritable palaces, and not surpassed by any other institutions of the kind in the world. The Misericordia has a fund whose value is more than $7,000,000. Besides these two great hospitals, we may mention at Rio, those of the Fraternities of S. Francisco da Penitencia, the Carmelites and S. Francisco de Paula, and that of the Portuguese Benevolent Society. There are also in the capital an asylum for foundlings, an asylum for orphans and an asylum for indigents.

The sailors of the vessels of all nations are treated gratuitously in the hospitals of the Misericordia.

The provinces possess establishments similar to those of the capital, and the number of charitable, benevolent and mutual aid societies is very considerable.

In the capital of the Empire and those of the provinces there are houses of correction and detention destined to convicts or those in course of trial. The first in importance of these is that of Rio de Janeiro, managed under the Auburn system, and with a capacity for 800 convicts. Next in importance come those of S. Paulo, Pernambuco and Bahia. We may mention besides the penal colony of the island of Fernando de Noronha, and the seven military training colonies on the banks of the Tocantins and the Araguaya.

III.

The public revenue comprises :—
1st. Municipal revenues, the product of taxation, having regard to the district of the capital of the Empire, levied by the Parliament and Central Government, and in the provinces by the provincial Legislative Assemblies, at suggestion of the municipalities. 2d. The provincial revenues, established by the same provincial Assemblies, with the sanction of the presidents or governors. 3d. The general revenues of the Empire, coming from taxes voted by the Chamber of Deputies and the Senate, and approved by the Emperor.

The general revenues of the Empire for the fiscal year 1831-32, the first of the present reign, amounted to $6,032,620.80. For the year 1840–41, the first after the majority of the Emperor, they had risen to $8,807,708.34.

Since that time the revenues have continued to increase rapidly as may be seen by the following figures :

1862–63.................	$26,104,778.28
1872–73.................	58,957,234.02
1882–83........	69,104,905.38

BUDGET FOR THE YEAR 1883–84. *

RECEIPTS.		EXPENDITURES.	
	Milreis.†		*Milreis.*
Customs........................ 93,709,800		Ministry of the Empire................. 9,777,309	
Duties on Navigation, Docks and Light Houses.......	400,000	" " Justice...................... 7,278,461	
Internal Revenues.		" " Foreign Affairs.............. 822,907	
Railroads.............. 13,140,000		" " Navy................. 11,262,960	
Telegraphs............... 900,000		" " War......................14,657,212	
Post Offices 1,500,000		" " Agriculture, Commerce and	
Stamps 5,000,000		Public Works........ 25,502,106	
Real Estate.............. 3,500,000 }..35,395,600		" " Finances................... 60,044,105	
Taxes on Industries and Professions 3,400,000			
Taxes on Sales of Property. 4,000,000		Total..............130,185,060	
Various Taxes...... 3,955,600			
Extraordinary Receipts.................. 1,410,000		Or in dollars......................$70,299,932.40	
Special Receipts....................... 1,200,000			
Total.................132,115,400			
Or in dollars..................... $71,342,316.00			

PUBLIC DEBT AND ASSETS OF THE STATE.

PUBLIC DEBT:
    1. Foreign Indebtedness (£19,036,500)............................... $91,376,341.92
    2. Domestic Indebtedness :

Consolidated Debt...............$219,045,276.00 ⎫	
Debt prior to 1827............... 169,541.10 ⎪	
Deposits, Orphan Funds, etc..... 28,661,187.42 ⎬	374,610,003.66
Treasury Bonds........ .... 25,191,812.16 ⎪	
Paper Money (Government Notes). 101,542,186.98 ⎭	

Total........$465,986,345.58

Let us remark here that, had it not been for the war with Paraguay which lasted five years and cost Brazil $340,200,000, the public debt would not now exceed $100,000,000, the interest of the debt considered.

The assets of the State consisted, in March, 1883, besides arrearages ($7,240,235.22) of a debt from the Republic of Uruguay of a total value of $8,748,071.46, and a debt from Paraguay amounting to $130,440.24. In addition, Paraguay is bound to indemnify Brazil for the expenses of the war.

The public force is composed of the Army, the Navy, the Police and the National Guard.

The armies of land and of sea are recruited by voluntary enlistment or by the drawing of lots. In extraordinary circumstances, or in case of threatening complications, the Government has the right to increase the effective force of the Army to 32,000 men, and, in case of war being declared, the number may be increased according to the necessities of the case, as happened in the last war (1864–70), when Brazil had for some time under arms as many as 80,000 men, forming the army corps which operated in the south of Paraguay and in Matto Grosso, the divisions guarding the frontiers of Rio Grande do Sul, and the garrisons of the interior.

---

* Proposition and Report presented to Parliament, in May, 1883, by the Minister of Finance.

† The milreis of Brazil is equivalent to about fifty-four cents when at par.

The regular effective force of the Army in time of peace is composed as follows :

Generals	29
Staff of Engineers, Chaplains and Sanitary Corps	451
Battalion of Engineers	800
Artillery	2,624
Cavalry	2,760
Infantry	8,624
Total	**15,288**

The Police force has an effective of 10,792, foot and horse.

The National Guard in 1881 was composed of 945,660—infantry, cavalry and artillery—of whom 691,384 formed the active and 254,276 the reserve. A law of 1873 abolished, except for the provincial frontiers, the garrison and police service imposed upon the National Guard, which was organized only for the national defence and the maintenance of public order in extraordinary circumstances. The Government is at present carefully reorganizing this militia, which rendered great service in the wars which Brazil has been obliged to carry on in the La Plata and in Paraguay since the beginning of the century. In time of war it is the National Guard that furnishes nearly all the fine cavalry of the Brazilian army in front of the enemy.

The Navy comprises fifty-eight vessels, of which fourteen are iron-clads, and the others frigates, corvettes and gun-boats. There is, besides, a number of torpedo boats. The fighting fleet intended for the high seas is composed of ten iron-clads, one frigate, seven corvettes, fifteen gun-boats, two transports, eight torpedo boats and one brig. Among these are included the two great iron-clads built in London, the *Riachuelo* and the *Aquidaban*. Next to these two iron-clads in importance are the *Solimões*, the *Javary*, and the *Sete de Setembro*. On the rivers Uruguay, Paraguay, Amazon and the lakes Mirim and dos Patos, Brazil has flotillas composed of small steamers, among which some iron-clads which did service in the war against the Dictator of Paraguay. The number of guns carried by the fleet is about 200.

The marine is composed of :

Generals (one Admiral, two Vice-Admirals, four Chiefs of Squadron and eight Chiefs of Division)	15
Officers of the First Class	384
" " Sanitary Corps	79
" " Pay Department	95
Guardians	92
Mechanics	188
Corps of Imperial Marines	3,000
Naval Battalion	600
Naval Apprentices	1,500
Artisans and Military Apprentices	173
Scholars of the Naval School	57
" " " College	86
Total	**6,269**

Summary :

Regular Army (on peace footing)	15,288
Police Force	10,792
National Guard, active	691,384
" " reserve	254,276
	971,730
Marine	6,269
Grand Total	**977,999**

There are naval arsenals at Rio de Janeiro, Bahia, Pernambuco, Maranhão and Matto Grosso ; and in these arsenals nearly all the vessels of the Brazilian navy, including iron-clads, have been constructed. During the Paraguayan War the arsenal at Rio displayed admirable activity. In August, 1867, the Admiral of the fleet asked for six monitors to force the passage of Humaitá, and in six months they were built and the passage was effected on the 19th of February following.

The arsenals of war are six in number, situated at Rio de Janeiro, Pará, Pernambuco, Bahia, Rio Grande do Sul and Matto Grosso. At Rio and in the provinces where there is an arsenal, there are also pyrotechnic laboratories. At Estrella, in the Province of Rio de Janeiro, and at Coxipó, in Matto Grosso, are powder factories. That at Estrella frequently produces more than 160,000 kilogrammes annually. At Ypanema, in the Province of S. Paulo, the Ministry of Public Works has a factory which furnishes all sorts of projectiles, iron and steel cannon, polished weapons and the metallic pieces needed by arsenals, both cast and forged, besides material for the railroads and Government workshops.

For military instruction, there are the Naval College, the Naval School, the Military Schools of Rio de Janeiro and of Porto Alegre, to which are attached preparatory departments. the general school of Instruction in Firing, at Campo Grande, the Regimental Schools and Depots of Artillery Scholars and Naval Scholars.

The libraries of the Army and Navy, at Rio de Janeiro, have already been mentioned, and we may add that in the provinces other libraries for the use of the garrisons exist.

At Rio are published the *Army Review* and the *Naval Review*, conducted by the officers of the two services.

In the bay of Rio is an asylum for invalid officers and soldiers of the Army, and a marine invalid asylum.

His Imperial Highness the Prince Gaston d'Orleans, Count d'Eu, with the rank of Marshal, was commander-in-chief of the Army, when its latest triumphs put an end to the war with Paraguay. He is at present commandant in chief of the artillery. The great centres of garrison are Rio de Janeiro and the frontiers of the Rio Grande do Sul and Matto Grosso. Twenty military posts, in addition to the disciplinary colonies already spoken of, have been established near the frontiers and in the interior ; designed to serve as centres of population in territory as yet uninhabited.

Post Offices.—Brazil is a member of the Postal Union. The general direction of postal affairs belongs to the Ministry of Agriculture, Commerce and Public Works.

Number of Post Offices and letters forwarded :

<pre>
1880—1,461 Post Offices............29,798,600 letters forwarded.
1882—1,610   " 35,845,869   "   "   *
</pre>

Telegraphs.—The Empire is connected with Europe by a sub-marine cable. Other cables connect the principal cities of the coast from Pará to Rio Grande do Sul, with a prolongation to the La Plata. Telegraphic land lines belong to the lines of railroads which they serve, or to the State. The Government lines in the years 1873, 1876 and 1882, were of the following extent :

<pre>
                                              Kilometres.   Kilometres.
1873—length of lines, 3,469 ; length of wires, 5,180 ; offices, 64.
1876—   "   "   5,151 ;   "   "   8,523 ;   "   87.
1882—   "   "   7,420 ;   "   " 13,250 ;   "   136.†
</pre>

Adding to the 7,420 kilometres of Government lines, 5,000 kilometres of lines belonging to the railroads, it will be seen that Brazil has a total of 12,420 kilometres of land lines of telegraph. The difficulties in establishing these lines and in maintaining them have been and are still great, because, to a great extent they traverse virgin forests and uninhabited lands.‡

The general direction of telegraphs is attached to the Department of Agriculture, Commerce and Public Works.

Telephones.—Lines of telephone have been established recently in Rio de Janeiro, Petropolis, and the principal commercial cities. In the capital, besides the public establishments and commercial houses, the hotels, restaurants, theatres, and many private residences, have been connected by the telephone, even in the farthest suburbs and on the surrounding mountains.

Street Railways.—All the important cities of Brazil have lines of street railways, more or less numerous, according to the needs of the population, and ancient omnibuses have quite disappeared.

Railroads.—The construction of railroads has been very actively pushed since 1871. In 1867 Brazil contained only 601 kilometres of railroad. At the commencement of 1883 the total extent of its lines was :

<pre>
Railroads in operation.................. ....4,865 kilometres.
    "   "   construction 2,489   "
                                 Total......................7,354   "
</pre>

At the time of this writing (May, 1884), Brazil possesses, certainly, 5,000 kilometres of railroads in operation.‖ Some of these lines have been constructed by foreign companies, but the greater part are the work of Brazilian companies and engineers. Thus, the Province of S. Paulo, which has a complete network of railroads, has only one, the central line from Santos to Jundiahy, constructed by a foreign company. All the rest have been built with Brazilian capital and by native engineers.

Roads.—Although the system of roads is not yet as much developed as the large territory of the Empire demands, communications are already supplied, for the more important districts, by broad roadways well kept up, some of which will hold comparison with the best national highways of Europe. Among these may be mentioned the magnificent roadway from Petropolis to Juiz de Fora.

Canals.—Brazil has few canals. The river system, the roads and railroads, render almost unnecessary the use of canals. All the existing ones are possessed of only a local importance—such as those of Campos and Macahé, of Cacimbas, of Magó and Itaguahy, in the Province of Rio de Janeiro ; Varadouro, in that of S. Paulo ; Coqueiros, Arapapahy and Mearim, in that of Maranhão ; Paxim, in the Province of Sergipe, and Ceará-Mirim and Trahyry, in that of Rio Grande do Norte.

<hr>

* 1883:—1,678 Post Offices, 36,767,325 letters forwarded.

† 1883:—length of lines 7,820 k. 912 m. ; length of wires 13,651 k. 768 m. ; offices 139.

‡ Notwithstanding those difficulties, the comparison between the interruptions of the telegraphic service through the land lines and those occasioned by the breaking of the coastwise cables of the Western & Brazilian Company, shows a great advantage in favor of the land lines, almost all built on iron posts and kept in excellent condition. In fact, the telegraph land lines of the Government of Brazil can only be compared with the best in this country or in Europe, both in their construction and operation.

‖ The last Report of the Department of Agriculture, Commerce and Public Works (1884) furnishes the following data :
Railroads in operation... 5,600 k. 846 m.
    "   "   construction ....2,875 k. 037 m.
                                 Total......................8,475 k. 883 m.

Navigation Lines along the Coast and on the Rivers.—The coast navigation employs twenty-eight lines of steamers, belonging, for the most part, to Brazilian companies. They receive subsidies from the Government, amounting altogether to the annual sum of more than $2,500,000. On nearly all the great rivers which run through inhabited territory, and on the lakes dos Patos, Mirim and Mangaba, there are steamboat lines, some of which are subsidized by the General Government or by the provinces.

In regard to foreign communications, there are steamship lines between Brazil and London, Southampton, Liverpool, Bordeaux, Havre, Marseilles, Lisbon, Barcelona, Genoa, Naples, Antwerp, Hamburg, Bremen, the United States, Canada, the Republics of Uruguay, Argentine, Paraguay, Chili and Peru, St. Vincent and Dakar, in Africa, and New Zealand. The steamships of these lines touch at Santos, Rio, Victoria, Bahia, Maceió, Pernambuco, Ceará, Maranhão, Pará, Serpa and Manáos, the last three of which are situated in the valley of the Amazon.

Docks and Basins.—Several concessions for the establishment of docks have been granted by the Government. Those of Rio de Janeiro already in service, are well known to foreign commerce. The magnificent basins of the navy, at Rio de Janeiro, may be mentioned. These are cut in the rock on the island das Cobras, in front of the arsenal.

Light-Houses.—The system of light-houses is not yet complete, but the Government is constantly increasing their number, and already they may be found at the approaches to the frequented harbors and at the points dangerous to navigation.

Quite recently, December 2, 1883, the electric light has been adopted for the fine light-house on the island Rasa, well known to navigators, near the entrance to the harbor of Rio de Janeiro.

IV.

Commerce.—Proportion of the commerce of Brazil with the other nations.—Principal articles of export and import.—Table of Brazilian exportation.—Commercial movement of the port of Rio de Janeiro.—Industry.—Agriculture.

We have already said that the ports of Brazil have been open to foreign commerce since 1808, at the arrival of the Royal Family of Bragança. Before that time all commerce had been carried on through the medium of the ports of Portugal, and the amount of imports and exports together never passed 22,600,000 milreis. Since 1808 exchanges have been rapidly developed, and now the annual value of the maritime commerce is more than 500,000,000 milreis.

The statistic tables of the Ministry of Finance at Rio de Janeiro, show that since 1839 the maritime foreign and inter-provincial commerce has grown at the annual rate of 20.67 per cent.

France, the country in Europe where commerce has most rapidly developed, has reached a mean annual rate of increase of only 10.2 per cent.

The following tables show the amount of the commerce of Brazil, inclusive of the precious metals and exclusive of the commerce in transit:

FOREIGN COMMERCE.

	IMPORTATION.	EXPORTATION.	TOTAL.
1870-71	137,264,000 milreis	166,949.400 milreis	304,213,400 milreis
1871-72	158,318,000 "	193,418,900 "	351,736,900 "
1872-73	156,730,600 "	215,893,100 "	372,623,700 "
1879-80	172,744,300 "	221,928,800 "	394,673,100 "
1880-81	180,458,700 "	233,567,700 "	414,026,400 "
1881-82	184,113,300 "	216,709,800 "	400,823,100 "

INTER-PROVINCIAL COMMERCE.

	IMPORTATION.	EXPORTATION.	TOTAL.
1879-80	105,149,500 milreis	75,563,300 milreis	180,712,800 milreis
1880-81	78,953,300 "	76,890,300 "	155,843,600 "
1881-82	91,428,300 "	83,471,100 "	174,899,400 "

Thus, in sum, the total value of maritime commerce, both foreign and inter-provincial, commerce in transit excluded, has risen in these late years to:

	IMPORTATION.	EXPORTATION.	TOTAL.
1879-80	277,893,800 milreis	297,492,100 milreis	575,385,900 milreis
1880-81	259,412,000 "	310,458,000 "	569,870,000 "
1881-82	275,541,600 "	300,180,900 "	575,722,500 "

To this total of foreign maritime commerce, the different countries have contributed in the following proportions:

		IMPORTATION.	EXPORTATION.	TOTAL REDUCED.
1.	Great Britain	51.47%	45.30%	48.38%
2.	France	19.49	13.46	16.48
3.	United States	4.67	20.90	12.78
4.	La Plata States	9.13	4.75	6.94
5.	Portugal	5.01	4.73	4.87
6.	Germany and Austria	5.21	3.43	4.32
7.	Spain	1.49	1.41	1.45
8.	Russia, Sweden and Norway	0.33	2.44	1.39
9.	Belgium	1.51	0.64	1.07
10.	Italy	0.44	0.81	0.63
11.	Chili and other Pacific countries	0.49	0.71	0.60
12.	Denmark	0.19	0.88	0.53
13.	Holland	0.15	0.03	0.09
14.	Other countries	0.42	0.51	0.47
		100.00%	100.00%	100.00%

Principal articles of Importation into Brazil.—Cotton, woolen, linen and silk fabrics, wines, liquors, beer, flour, rice, lard, olive oil, codfish, butter, cheese, salt, spices, tea, preserves, vegetables and fruits of Europe, coal, iron and other useful metals, rails and other materials for railroads and steam navigation, agricultural and industrial machinery, iron implements, fire-arms, petroleum, pine, pitch, cement, candles, bagging, crockery, porcelain and glass, mirrors, furniture and carpeting, pianos and other musical instruments, paper, books, chemical preparations, medicines, mineral waters, boots and shoes, hats, gold in coin, hardware, cutlery, clocks and watches, jewelry, perfumery, laces, clothing, fashions and articles of Paris.

The import trade is carried on by Brazilians and foreigners. Among the latter the English and Portuguese come first, and next the Germans, French and Italians.

Principal articles of Export.—Coffee, sugar, cacao, meal of mandioca, tapioca, mate (Paraguay tea), Brazil nuts, salted meats, rum from the sugar-cane, molasses, ipecacuanha, urucu, India-rubber, raw cotton, tobacco, rosewood and other woods, hides, furs, hair, skins, wools. horns, tallow, gold, diamonds and other precious stones,

The following table shows the amount and value of the chief articles of Brazilian exportation in the year 1839-40, and in the three last years for which we have been able to obtain official figures—those of 1879-80, 1880-81 and 1881-82. It will be seen from this how much the production has increased since 1840 :

EXPORTATIONS OF BRAZIL.	QUANTITY.				VALUE (MILREIS).			
	1839-40.	1879-80.	1880-81.	1881-82.	1839-40.	1879-80.	1880-81.	1881-82.
Coffee..... ...(kilogr.)	83,037,374	157,036,317	219,569,022	244,888,012	20,176,363	126,259,900	126,134,000	104,752,700
Sugar........ .. "	81,452,317	216,461,155	161,258,398	246,769,276	10,887,444	31,333,760	25,935,100	36,445,000
India Rubber... "	417,862	6,880,482	6,722,638	6,840,210	257,590	12,242,500	11,855,700	12,005,400
Raw Cotton .... "	10,260,394	11,356,264	12,710,261	21,916,228	3,984,425	5,186,700	5,114,600	9,662,300
Hides and Skins. "	8,862,517	25,263,685	21,537,201	20,245,102	3,017,897	8,979,900	8,269,500	7,894,100
Tobacco........ "	4,350,714	24,539,572	19,900,188	23,046,845	657,443	7,660,800	7,553,600	7,912,300
Mate (Paraguay Tea)........ "	2,549,303	14,063,731	14,275,036	15,952,872	226,778	2,521,900	2,702,100	2,697,800
Brazil Nuts..... "	....	6,738,580	5,698,505	4,985,200	....	1,473,800	1,112,700	1,052,000
Diamonds....(grammes)	2,275	13,546	19,519	11,646	186,800	1,007,100	1,307,500	861,200
Cacao..........(kilogr.)	2,958,360	1,539,954	1,122,649	1,969,789	40,274	1,002,500	704,600	985,000
Meal of Mandioca "	1,088,790	4,158,659	2,473,592	3,127,614	137,408	335,000	267,000	107,000
Rum of Sugar Cane (litres)	6,036,697	3,308,328	2,704,934	2,120,931	625,775	336,500	309,400	281,200
Wool...........(kilogr.)	166,344	420,144	327,269	345,800	23,352	138,800	142,500	151,200
Hair.......... "		478,429	410,773	458,450		309,500	275,800	334,100
Various Products........	....	....	....	....	2,598,471	23,160,200	41,583,600	31,567,000
Total....	....	....	....	....	42,524,020	221,948,800	233,567,700	216,709,800

The following is the movement of shipping for the port of Rio de Janeiro during the last two years :

YEARS.		VESSELS ENTERED.		VESSELS LEFT.	
		Number of Vessels.	Tonnage.	Number of Vessels.	Tonnage.
1882	Foreign..............	1,288	1,197,671	1,164	1,140,439
	Coastwise..............	1,439	400,130	1,642	535,558
		2,727	1,597,801	2,806	1,675,997
1883	Foreign..............	1,218	1,220,332	1,067	1,207,821
	Coastwise	1,414	454,739	1,588	540,891
		2,632	1,675,071	2,655	1,748,712

Although Brazil is not yet, properly speaking, a manufacturing country, it has, in this respect, made great progress, and is far in advance of the other South American countries. There are in the capital and in the provinces important factories, many of which are provided with steam power, and which give employment to many workmen. Some of them, by the perfection of their apparatus and the excellence of their products, may vie with those of the most advanced nations, as is proved by the numerous premiums obtained at the international expositions. The Government has, at different times, granted subsidies to manufacturing establishments of more than usual importance, and has at all times encouraged useful enterprises.

In the interior are produced, on a large scale, sugar, sugar-cane rum, liquors from coffee, cacao and other substances, vinegar, beer, wine of cajú and other fruits, and, in the southern provinces, grape wine, flour and meal of mandioca, Indian corn and wheat, tapioca and other farinaceous foods, the mate, guaraná, oils for burning and for table, butter, cheese, preserves, chocolate, meats in brine and dried, tobacco in rolls, cigars and cigarettes, extracts of meat and concentrated soups, fish dried and in pickle, soap, candles of tallow, wax or carnaúba (*Copernicia cerifera*), India-rubber, paste, dried and tanned hides, common fabrics for coffee and sugar bags, fine cloths for garments, ropes, tow, and pottery for household purposes.

There exist, besides, in the capital of the Empire and in those of the provinces, a great number of factories and workshops for the manufacture of articles which formerly came only from abroad. Such, at Rio de Janeiro, are the factories for chemical products, mirrors, optical instruments, instruments of navigation, surveying and surgery, factories of hats of straw, felt or silk, of boots and shoes, clothing, oil cloths, carpets, enameled leather and morocco, glass, crockery ware, fine and common, artificial stone, sash, mosaics, dye-stuffs, common and artistic furniture, carriage work, railway and horse cars, agricultural machines and implements, oils, soap, candles, distillation, beer, plain and colored papers, varnish, card-board, snuff, cigars and cigarettes, artificial marble, diamond cutting, gloves, cloth and feather flowers, many of which have obtained medals abroad, which testify to the excellence of these products. In Rio de Janeiro and its suburbs forty-five quarries give employment to more than a thousand stone-cutters. In several capitals, and in different cities and towns, there are, as at Rio, workshops for jewelry, clock-making, saddlery, rope-making, tinware, clothing, cloth and feather flowers, laces, crochet and needle-work, and leather-work. These last are manufactured with rare excellence in Rio Grande do Sul, Paraná, S. Paulo and Minas Geraes.

Spinning mills and cloth manufactories are already very numerous, the most important being the factory "Brazil Industrial," near Rio, at the village of Macacos.

Among the manufactories established at Rio may be mentioned twenty-four foundries of machinery, of iron, bronze, brass and copper, remarkable for their outfit and the excellence of their work. There are also in the provinces a number of foundries. In the harbor of Rio are naval workshops belonging to private companies, where large vessels can be built.

Brazil belongs to the International Union for the protection of property in manufactures, on the terms of the convention signed at Paris March 20th, 1883.

Agriculture is the most important source of national wealth in Brazil. The soil still covered, in great part, with virgin forests, is of wonderful fertility, so that its cultivators find in it ample remuneration for their labors. Thus, the yield of the crops of wheat and rye, which in Europe is in the ratio of twenty to one of seed, in Asia eight to twelve, in the Argentine Republic fifteen to twenty-five, is in Brazil from thirty to sixty, and even seventy, in some parts of the Province of Rio Grande do Sul. Indian corn, as we have already stated, yields an average of two hundred for one, and in some places three or four hundred. Rice yields as much as one thousand for one; beans from eighty to two hundred, in the Province of Paraná. Lands are mentioned yielding :

```
Per hectare ....................... 4,266 to 4,742 kilogrammes of cotton.
  "        "      ...............................3,554      "      " coffee.
  "        "      ...............................7,344      "      " tapioca.
  "        "      ...............................9,390 litres      " Indian corn.
  "        "      ...............................18,730  "         " mandioca.
```

The vegetation of the tropics, so varied and vigorous, is met with on the coast, on the plains, and the low regions of the northern and central provinces ; while in a great portion of these very provinces, the elevation of the soil, as soon as one passes the mountain chain parallel with the coast, and the vast plateau of the interior, permit the cultivation of all the fruits, vegetables and cereals of the temperate zones. In the Provinces of Paraná, Santa Catharina and Rio Grande do Sul, situated beyond the tropic, and much further from the equator, the soil produces everywhere, in the mountainous regions as well as in the plains and litoral, the plants of southern Europe, and presents conditions extremely favorable for the culture of all the productions of the temperate zones. While in certain localities are cultivated cotton, sugar-cane, coffee, tobacco, cacao and vanilla, tea, and all the plants of Asia ; in others, sometimes close neighbors, one finds productive plantations of wheat, barley, rye, the vine, pears, apples and peaches.

Says the scientist Agassiz : "By reason of its climate and geographical situation, the zones of vegetation are not so definitely marked in Brazil as in other countries ; it would, however, be possible to divide the country, in an agricultural sense, into three grand regions: the first, extending from the boundaries of Guiana to Bahia, along the great rivers, is particularly characterized by its wild forest products, India-rubber, cacao, vanilla, salsaparilla, and an immense variety of gums, resins, barks, textile fibres, yet unknown to the world's commerce, and to which might be easily added spices, the monopoly in which, up to the present time, has belonged to the Indian Archipelago ; the second region, from Bahia to Santa Catharina, is that of coffee ; the third, from Santa Catharina to Rio Grande do Sul, inclusive, adding the high plateaus of the interior, is that of the cereals ; and, in connection with their culture, the raising of cattle. Rice, which grows readily throughout Brazil, and cotton, which everywhere produces well, bind these three zones together ; sugar and tobacco fill the gaps, and complete the chain."

The large planters of Brazil devote themselves almost exclusively to the cultivation of coffee, sugar-cane and cotton. The products of these three branches make up more than two-thirds of the amount of Brazilian exports, as has already been shown in the article on commerce, where may also be remarked the growing importance of rubber production in the rich valley of the Amazon.

Flax culture, in the Provinces of Paraná and Rio Grande do Sul, gives better results than in Europe. In other provinces the stalks of a great number of plants furnish textile fibres, that in whiteness and strength are destined to rival flax.

At the time of the civil war in the United States, cotton culture developed prodigiously in Brazil. Without giving up other cultivation, the Brazilian planters succeeded in exporting annually enormous quantities of cotton, sufficient to meet the deficiency caused by that war. The Province of S. Paulo, where a single stalk of cotton had never before been planted, those of Alagôas, Parahyba do Norte and Ceará, where its culture had been abandoned, succeeded, with those of Pernambuco and Maranhão, in increasing, in a short time, their production five fold. At the Universal Exposition at Paris, in 1867, a special premium was awarded to Brazil, whose people, by their energy, had succeeded in supplying the European markets with an article of prime necessity.

Tobacco grows spontaneously in Brazil, and its culture tends to improve in methods and extent ; that of Bahia is the best.

The grape vine thrives in S. Paulo, Paraná, Rio Grande do Sul, and in certain districts of the Provinces of Rio de Janeiro and Minas Geraes; but the Brazilian wines are all consumed in the country, and do not figure among the exports

The seringueira (*Siphonia elastica*), which supplies the rubber, is a wild tree, a native of the forests which cover the valley of the Amazon. Its cultivation was commenced some years since at Pará. This rich product of the Brazilian forests has established its reputation in all the markets of the world, where it obtains the best prices, as being the best rubber in the world.

The mandioca (*Manhiot utilissima*), of which in Brazil there are more than thirty varieties, succeeds in nearly all the lands of the torrid and temperate zones: but especially in dry, loose and sandy soils. It is from the root of this plant that the celebrated tapioca of Brazil is made, also meal of mandioca, different pastes, starch, a sauce known as tucupy, and alcoholic drinks. Its cultivation requires so little care, the different processes to which the roots are submitted are so simple and cheap, that, even if the present prices should decline one-half, tapioca and the flours would still yield a great profit to its cultivators.

In several of the provinces hop culture has given good results, and a large part of the production is used in the country in the making of beer. Pomoculture, horticulture, and gardening, have made great advances in the last few years.

Nearly all the soil of Brazil, and particularly that of the provinces between Rio Grande do Norte and Rio de Janeiro, inclusive, produces the sugar-cane abundantly, and plantations of it frequently produce well for sixteen to twenty years. In Matto Grosso plantations of forty years are still quite vigorous. The cane reproduces itself, in this province, with such rapidity along the rivers, that it is frequently necessary to thin out the plantations, according to the testimony of the Italian traveller Bossi. Even in silicious soils the cultivation of the cane is profitable, and of all these are most uncongenial to its growth. On lands newly opened it is not unusual to harvest, at the end of fifteen months, 100,000 kilogrammes of cane per hectare, and raise at the same time, on the same land, crops of leguminous plants. A single laborer, with the aid of the plow, can take care of two hectares planted in cane, and realize an annual profit of $800, selling the cane at the rate of $4.00 per thousand kilogrammes. Fourteen provinces have recently obtained privileges for fifty-one central factories for the making of sugar and rum. For the establishment of these factories the Government guarantees an interest of six or seven per cent. on the capital invested, which amounts to about $10,500,000. The subject of establishing central factories for coffee is also discussed.

Cattle raising is profitably pursued in almost all the provinces, especially in the vast pasture grounds of the interior, in Minas Geraes, Bahia, Piauhy and the noble plains of Rio Grande do Sul, Paraná and S. Paulo. The herds, needing almost no attention, are left to take care of themselves.

Brazil has received the name of the Land of Coffee, and certainly it deserves the appellation, since it produces fifty-five per cent. of the world's total production.

This total production is at present 660,000,000 kilogrammes per annum, and is thus distributed:

Production of Brazil..............360,000,000 kilogrammes.
Production of all other countries......300,000,000 "

Total World's production........660,000,000 kilogrammes.

And yet, in 1800, Brazil exported only 13 bags of coffee! In 1817, it exported 66,085 bags; in 1820, 97,498; in 1830, 484,222; 1,037,981 in 1840, and 3,765,122 in 1876.

To-day the annual production of Brazil is more than 6,000,000 bags of 60 kilogrammes each.

COFFEE.

EXTRACT FROM A MONOGRAPH WRITTEN

–BY–

Mr. de SANT' ANNA NERY,

Member of the Parisian Press.

1883.

COFFEE.

I.

GENERAL CONSIDERATIONS.

SUMMARY :—*Coffee.*—*Different varieties of coffee plants.*—*Brazil the country where the cultivation of coffee has most extended itself.*—*The production of all other countries together not equal to that of Brazil alone.*—*Methods of cultivating coffee.*—*Brazilian coffees studied at the Conservatoire des Arts et Métiers at Paris, by General Morin, Prof. Péligot, Dr. Laborie and Mr. Henri.*—*Manner of preparing coffee.*—*Opinion of Dr. Peunetier on Brazilian coffees.*—*Chemical analysis of coffee.*—*Brazilian coffee the richest in caffeine.*—*Analysis of Brazilian coffees by Dr. Ludwig, director of the Chemical Laboratory of the Faculty of Medicine at Vienna.*—*Opinion of Dr. Lucien Martin on the use of coffee in the army and navy.*—*The suppression of alcoholism only to be accomplished by the general use of coffee.*—*The abuse of coffee not to be dreaded as that of spirituous liquors or of tobacco.*—*Hygienic properties of coffee.*—*May be employed in medication.*—*Its adulterations in Europe attributable to the high duties.*—*Measures recently adopted in England to prevent adulterations.*

Coffee is a native of Ethiopia, Yemen and Arabia. It is a shrub, belonging to the family of the *Rubiaceæ*, flourishing only on sloping grounds, and demanding a climate whose temperature ranges from 10° to 30° Centigrade.

With respect to the *planting* and *cultivation* of coffee, the Dutch may claim to have been the true pioneers, as the Turks have been most instrumental in extending its *use*.

There are several varieties of the coffee plant, viz. :

ARABIAN COFFEE : Moka, Myrtle, Aden and Bastard.

MOORISH COFFEE : Marron of Reunion.

MONROVIAN COFFEE : Coffee of Gabon.

LAURINE COFFEE.

COFFEE AMARELLO : Wild shrub with berries yellow or *amarellas*, the richest of all in caffeine, found in the forests of Botucatá, in the Province of S. Paulo, Brazil.

COFFEE VERMELHO OR RED : The ordinary coffee of Brazil. Brazil is the country where coffee is most extensively cultivated ; it is there it seems to flourish most vigorously, and it is there the richest plantations are found. Colombia, Guatemala, Venezuela, Nicaragua, San Salvador, Costa Rica and Mexico also furnish a certain amount ; but the production of all these countries together is not one-third of that supplied by Brazil.*

A practical classification will admit ten or twelve sub-divisions of numerous varieties, whose prices are as various as their quality, their aroma and their origin.

This distinction is very essential, and we will now consider the correct nomenclature of the different kinds of coffee offered by commerce to the world's consumption.

AMERICA.

BRAZIL :—Rio de Janeiro, (*Rio, Rio Lavado, Capitania, Andarahy*) ; Santos, (*Santos, Santos Lavado*) ; Minas Geraes ; Bahia, (*Bahia, B. Caravellas, B. Muritiba, B. Valença, B. Maragogipe*) ; Ceará ; Pernambuco ; Amazonas.

THE ANTILLES :—Hayti or St. Domingo (*St. Marc, Môle, Gonaïves, Santo Domingo, Port-de-Paix, Porto-Plata, Cap-Haïtien, Port-au-Prince, Jacmel, Jérémie, Aquin, Cayes*) ; Jamaica, (*J. Plantation, J. Ordinary*); Porto Rico ; Martinique ; Guadalupe (*L'Habitant, le Bonifieur*) ; Cuba, (*Santiago de Cuba, Havana*).

CENTRAL AMERICA :—Guatemala, (*G. Ordinary, G. Gragé*) ; Nicaragua ; Savanilla ; Costa Rica, (*C. Ordinary, C. Gragé*) ; Honduras ; San Salvador.

VENEZUELA :—Porto Cabello, (*P. Gragé*) ; Laguayra ; Maracaibo.

PERU :—Carabaya ; Huanaca.

BOLIVIA :—Yungas.

GUIANA :—Cayenne, (*Côte de Remire, Montagne d'Argent, Kaw, Oyac*).

---

* The total annual production at this time is 666,000 tons of 1,000 kilogrammes each, viz. :

Production of Brazil	300,000 tons.
" " all other countries	300,000 "
	666,000 tons.

AFRICA.

WESTERN AFRICA :—Madeira ; Cape Verde : Senegambia, (*Cazengo, Rio Nunez*) ; Gabon, (*Gabon, Benguela, Monrovia*) ; San Thomé, (*Principe*) ; Angola, (*Encoge, Cazengo*).

EASTERN AFRICA :—Island of Reunion, (*Bourbon pointed, B. Round ; varieties, Moka, Myrtle, Leroy, St. Leu, Moorish*) ; Mayotte ; Nossi-Bé ; Mozambique, (*Inhambane*) ; Madagascar, (*Tamatave*) ; Zanzibar, (*Moka Zanzibar*) ; Berber.

ARABIA :—Moka, (*Moka of Moka, Moka of Aden, Hodeidah, Kusma, Dejebi, Aden*).

ASIA.

INDIA :—Bombay, (*Bombay Moka*) ; Mangalore ; Mysore ; Malabar ; Wynaad ; Tellitcherry ; Nilgberries ; Salem ; Ceylon, (*Native Ceylon, Plantation Ceylon*).

INDIA BEYOND THE GANGES :—Cochin China ; Singapore.

INDIAN ARCHIPELAGO :—Java, (*Preanger, Demerary, Menado, Tagal, Malang, Solo, Tjilatjap, Samarang, Cheribon, Tenger, Kadoe, Pecalongan, Passaroean*) ; Palembang ; Padang ; Celebes, (*Paré-Paré, Boenge, Macassar*) ; Sumatra ; Luçon, (*Manilla, Zamboang*) ; Tahiti ; New Caledonia.

The coffee plants are set in quincunx order, on the slopes of slightly shaded hills, where the rainfall is not too great.

The plants are started in seed beds, and by the end of one year are strong enough to be transplanted in holes regularly disposed and about four metres apart. In Brazil it is only about the fourth year that the plant begins to produce ; but from that time forward the production goes on continually increasing. It then reaches a height of from three to five metres, with a circumference of 0.50 to 0.60 centimetres.* It comes into full bearing at the age of eight or nine years, and continues to produce for forty years, if care is taken to prune it and remove the dead branches.

In Brazil, for opening a coffee plantation, virgin and wooded lands are preferred, and the plants are in full bearing at the end of seven years. Land of this description having been selected, the trees are cut down and burned ; and the plantation once established, the plants are left to their natural growth ; care being taken, however, to protect them against weeds, which would otherwise speedily take possession of the plantation. It is well known that neither an intense heat nor intense cold is favorable to the coffee plant ; and in Brazil it succeeds, generally, only between the 18th and 20th parallels.

They consider in Brazil that an acre of land, properly prepared, should support about 450 coffee plants.

Before the decline in the coffee market during the last few years, and whose causes we will consider further on, the average return from each laborer, including women, children and old men, was about $340.†

Coffee is cultivated in Brazil from the Amazon River to the Province of S. Paulo, embracing about 20° of latitude. From the coast to the western limit of the Province of Matto-Grosso is 25° of longitude ; and the entire zone in which the culture of coffee may be carried comprises more than three million square kilometres.

It has been said, and perhaps with good reason, that the Brazilian planters do not prepare their products with as much skill and care as those of Ceylon and Java, and that consequently, the coffee of Brazil has a slight bitterness and earthy flavor. We would remark however, that this flavor is far from disagreeable, and besides, that it is considerably diminished if the coffee is kept one or two years before using—a precaution, too, which should be taken with all coffees. This defect, or this peculiarity, which all genuine coffees present, is very much appreciated by the coffee drinkers of North America.

We borrow from General Morin the results of the investigations undertaken by him at the Conservatoire des Arts et Métiers in conjunction with Mr. Péligot, the eminent professor of Chemistry. ‡ These eminent scientists agree in the opinion that coffee, like generous wines, need time for the development of its more exquisite qualities, and that it is age that makes good coffee.

The driest coffees, whose color is generally a pale yellow, have a weight density of about 500 grammes to the cubic centimetre, while those of a greenish appearance and which have not been gathered more than a year or two, have an average weight of 680 grammes, and sometimes more to the cubic centimetre without packing.

Now, since coffee is always sold by weight, it becomes to the interest of dealers to sell it in as green a state as possible, because the consumer would be unwilling to pay an increase in price corresponding to the diminution in weight consequent on long keeping.

So true is this that the dealers in even the very good coffees of the coast of Africa, called Zanzibar Mokas, are able to sell their coffees for the average price of five francs per kilogramme at the end of *two years'* keeping ; whereas, if they were perfectly dry they would be worth more than seven francs, taking into account the loss from drying.

The aroma of coffee is in the direct ratio of its desiccation by keeping.

It is possible that some day certain modes of treatment and manipulation may be found to take the place of the years now necessary, and allow us to enjoy our coffee in its full flavor.

---

* The average height of a Brazilian coffee tree is three metres, and the circumference 1.50 metre. Generally produces for twenty years.

†See *L'Empire du Brésil à l'Exposition de Philadelphie*, Rio de Janeiro, 1876, one volume with plates.

‡ See in the *Annales du Conservatoire des Arts et Métiers* the note on the *different varieties of coffee and especially on the coffees of Brazil* by *Gen. Morin*.

WEIGHT.—DENSITIES OF OLD COFFEES.

ORIGIN.	DATE OF CROP.	CONDITION OF THE GRAINS.	WEIGHT PER LIVRE.	NUMBER OF GRAINS TO THE DECILITRE.
Moka (*Amiral de Rigny*),	1828	Grains regular, fine.	500 grms.	510
Moka of Aden,	1874	Much mixed.	606 "	554
Zanzibar Moka,	1874	"	600 "	476
Java,	....	Regular large.	455 "	338
Reunion,	1869	Fine, pointed at the ends	630 "	488
Brazil,	1872	Regular large.	522 "	294
Brazil (*Rio*), { No. 16.	1867		460 "	300
No. 17.	1871 }	Regular large.	544 "	292
No. 18.	1872		586 "	354
Venezuela,	1865	Ovoid medium.	654 "	400
San Salvador,	1873	" "	662 "	...
Cochin China, }		Small.	614 "	544
Rio Nunez,		"	580 "	618
Nossi Bé,		Medium.	584 "	432
Nossi Bé (*Wild*), }	Very Dry.	Ovoid very small.	440 "	752
Gabon,		Large irregular.	490 "	336
Caledonia, }		Medium.	570 "	442
Ceylon,	Medium Dry.	Fine.	580 "	452
Brazil (*Espirito Santo*),	1875	Large (*artificially dried.*)	567 "	318

It will be seen from this table that the *Brazilian coffee* is the largest and most regular of all.
This coffee also appears to demand less time for desiccation than the others, since its weight density is:

For 8 years.............................. .... 4.60 grammes.
" 4 " .... 5.44 "
" 3 " .... 5.86 "

For one year, after artificial drying, its density is 567 grammes per litre; that is, Brazilian coffee is better suited for artificial drying, which, if practical and properly done, might give to coffee one year old the aroma and density of that of ten years.

The Brazilian planters ought to make special efforts in this direction, if they wish that in all the world's markets their coffees shall possess the best qualities.

In Brazil the gathering of the crop begins in April or May, and is prolonged sometimes even into November, owing to irregular ripening.

The proper preparation of coffee for drinking is also of much importance with respect to its quality, and a few hints in this respect will not be superfluous; inasmuch as there are very few families where they know how to prepare the beverage in a suitable and rational manner.

The coffee should be roasted but a few hours before being used; as coffee after being roasted sometimes secretes an oily substance which is changed by contact with the air and gives the coffee a bitter and disagreeable flavor.

It may be kept, at most, a day or two in a close vessel.

The roaster which is commonly employed is not objectionable, provided sudden motions and sharp shocks be avoided, and a lively but even fire of charcoal should be used.

By the action of the fire, the grains increase in size from one-half to three-fourths of their original dimensions, and the loss in weight varies with the degree of dryness of the grains, being from 13 to 18 per cent. in roasting until they become of a chestnut color. Roasted until the loss reached 20 per cent. it would be too oily and would stain paper.

The proper quantity for ordinary cups of one decilitre is 25 grains to a decilitre and a half of water, and the temperature of the water for the infusion should be a little below the boiling point.

Vessels of earthenware or porcelain alone should be used for the filters, and metals and steam devices rejected.

Gen. Morin, Mr. Péligot, Dr. Laborie, Mr. Heuzé of the *Société d' Agriculture*, Messrs. Bignon and Magny, the well known restaurateurs, experimented in 1875, by tasting the different coffees in use.

Their experiments were made in conditions not favorable to the coffees of Brazil; while the other coffees experimented with were very dry and had lost their green taste, the Brazilian coffee was of the current year's crop.

In spite of this genuine disadvantage, they found the Brazilian coffee excellent and assigned to it a very good rank in the general classification.

The experimenters divided the coffee, according to flavor and aroma, into three classes, which seem to us to be rational:

1. Dry coffees, having a very decided aroma, which admits of their being mixed.
2. Dry coffees, with less aroma, more mild, which can be used alone.
3. Green or undried coffees.

In the first of these classes, the Brazilian coffee two years old was able to compete with coffees of a much greater age; and was placed as 8th in the classification, with the note: "Very well handled, *very good*, not yet dry enough."

There were placed before it only five sorts of very old Moka, one of Martinique, and one of Ceylon, each three years old.

The coffee Amarello or yellow was judged as well handled, very good and very strong for mixing.

Mr. Péligot also determined that the coffee Amarello is much richer in caffeine than the Vermelho.

In the second category of dry, mild coffees, Brazilian coffee takes the second rank, next to the Saint Leu of Reunion. The coffees of Rio, S. Paulo, Campinas, Santos, Capitania, Espirito Santo, were judged as very well handled, very dry, *of a fresh and agreeable taste*.

In the provisional classification of green or young coffees, the Brazil incontestably takes the first rank ; and is, of all the coffees, the one that has less need of age to render it passably, if not quite good. It is this quality which gives it commercial superiority over the other coffees of the world.

The coffee of Minas Geraes was considered as having a strong, but good flavor, which would improve with age.

The following is the conclusion reached by Mr. Péligot and General Morin in regard to Brazilian coffees :

" Apart from the coffees of Arabia, Martinique and Reunion, which, indeed, constitute only about five per cent. of the total consumption of France, our commerce should give the preference to those of Brazil ; not only on account of the care with which they are handled, but also of their good qualities. French commerce and French consumers should, therefore, hope for the development and improvement of this production in that rich and fertile land."

Dr. Georges Pennetier, director of the *Muséum d'Histoire Naturelle* of Rouen, adds the following to the flattering and encouraging expressions which we have just cited :

" Certain of the Brazilian coffees have an aroma equal to that of Martinique, and the greater number of them, when sufficiently dry, are of a fresh and very pleasant flavor. They may be accepted by consumers as equal to those of Reunion, and seem to be superior to all others grown in other American countries."

The most recent chemical analyses of coffee give :

Water	as a mean,		.12
Cellulose	"		.34
Fatty matter	"	.10 to	.13
Glucose Dextrine	}		
Caffeic Acid	"	.15 to	.16
Citric Acid and other non-nitrogenous matter.	}		
Nitrogenous matter	}		.17
Caffeine, legumina	}		
Mineral substances	"	.06 to	.07

The fatty substances which give the odor to raw coffee are few in number.

The characteristic constituent is caffeine, an alkaloid discovered by Runger. It crystallizes in silky, white and odorless filaments, slightly bitter and volatile. It is very rich in nitrogen and possesses excellent alimentary properties, inasmuch as it contains 30% of its weight of nitrogen. It is the active principle of coffee and identical in composition with theine of tea, theobromine of cacao and guaranine of guaraná.

Mr. Vandencorput has found caffeine in the leaves of the coffee plant to the amount of two per cent.

Roasting effects a change in the chemical composition of coffee. The woody portion is partially decomposed and becomes brittle ; the dextrine and glucose are changed into a brown substance, bitter and soluble in water ; under the action of the heat, an oily principle, very aromatic and very volatile, called *caffeone*, is developed. The greater part of the caffeine remains, but a portion is decomposed, forming methylamine.

The amount of caffeine varies with the varieties of the coffee. In 500 grammes, subjected to analysis, there were found :

Coffee Amarello (Yellow Coffee) of Brazil	1.82	gramme.
Martinique	1.79	"
Alexandria	1.26	"
Java	1.26	"
Moka	1.06	"
Cayenne	1.00	"
Santo Domingo	0.89	"

Not only is the Brazilian coffee the richest in caffeine, but it is the one which contains most substances soluble in water—even as high as 45 %.

Quite recently, a young Brazilian physician, Dr. C. Teixeira, wishing to obtain a correct estimate of the exact value of the different qualities of coffee, had the happy idea of asking Dr. Ernst Ludwig, the learned director of the Laboratory of Chemistry of the Faculty of Medicine of Vienna, to make an analysis of two different sorts of Brazilian coffee which he gave him. Dr. Ludwig made the analysis, using the method of Dragendorff ; and the result of the analysis has demonstrated the superiority of the Brazilian coffee, with respect to the proportion of caffeine, over those of a different origin. It is superior to the Ceylon, wild and cultivated, to the Martinique, the Alexandria, Java, Moka, Cayenne and Santo Domingo. According to the analysis of Dr. Ludwig, which in this respect agrees to that of other celebrated chemists, the proportion of caffeine contained in Brazilian coffee varies from 1.16 to 1.75 %.

The chemical analysis which we have just given, indicates the principal effects which may be produced upon the organism by the use of coffee.

It stimulates thought, excites the imagination, arouses all the intellectual faculties and produces insomnia in the case of those not accustomed to its use.

Messrs. de Gasparin and Payen have established the fact that coffee drinkers need less aliments than those who do not ordinarily use it ; and these scientists have also given the causes which produce this phenomenon. They discovered that coffee, without having any direct nutritive properties, retards in an appreciable manner the processes of waste.

The poor, then, above all, laborers, soldiers and all persons whose food is scanty or poor, should use coffee.

In the countries where habitual use is made of beer and cider, coffee becomes a tonic of prime necessity.

Dr. Lucien Martin, in the journal *l'Hygiène Pratique*, devotes an admirable article to a demonstration of the happy results that may be secured by the rational employment of coffee in the army and navy. He shows that the suppression of alcohol can be accomplished only by the substitution for it of some liquid possessing the same properties without its bad results. Besides, taken at a warm temperature, its heat is beneficial to those exposed to cold, and the sugar which is taken with it, is a respiratory aliment of the first order.

"Coffee," says he, " is really indispensable to soldiers, not only to sustain, arouse and warm them, but also to preserve them from, or cure them of, a disease very common in camp or on the march, the diarrhœa, which exhausts and soon drags down the most vigorous. Coffee is then, most assuredly, the best of all hygienic preventives, and with it, one may have ever at hand an agreeable and efficient means of resistance to the intermittent fevers which are only too well known to us.

"A supplementary distribution of coffee, of which a decoction could be made with the unroasted grains, might take the place of the ration of sulphate of quinine, which, in summer and autumn, is allowed to the garrisons of certain posts. It would replace it all the more advantageously, because the soldier, in the belief that quinine is injurious to his stomach, is in no hurry to take it, but prefers to sell it to the citizens of the vicinity."

The logical conclusion from these considerations is the necessity of issuing to soldiers daily rations of at least 25 grammes of coffee. It would be well, too, if poor families could obtain the same amount, per head, of this almost necessary beverage, whose abuse is not to be dreaded, like that of alcohol or tobacco. Mr. Pouchet, in his *Traité élémentaire de botanique appliquée*, mentions a very curious case in this connection : "We have seen," says he, "in an inn at Lons-le-Bourg, at the foot of Mount Cenis, a good woman 116 years old, who had the habit of taking 25 to 30 cups of coffee per day." After this it is useless to cite the longevity of Voltaire.

In sum, coffee augments the activity of the functions of the brain, and retards the waste of the living tissues. Physicians may advantageously employ it against headaches, neuralgia, whooping-cough and intermittent fevers, and as a reagent to prevent narcotic poisonings [*]

But to produce these happy results, it is indispensable that the coffee be pure, and without injurious changes or adulterations ; it must not be taken from sickly plants or put into bags before being perfectly dry.

Ground coffee is especially exposed to numerous adulterations, being sometimes mixed with inferior sorts, damaged coffee, coffee grounds colored with caramel, and also chicory, roasted and adulterated.

The means of testing these ground coffees are within the reach of every one.

One has only to throw a pinch of this coffee into a cup of water. If a part of the powder floats and the rest sinks, while the water becomes immediately colored, the coffee has been adulterated.

Our chemical laboratories would do well to analyze and denounce these injurious preparations which are sold among us under the fair name of coffee. England has just set us the example. A body of important regulations, in relation to coffee and chicory, has just been announced. A special provision imposes a tax of half-penny per 112 grammes upon all vegetable substances which are mentioned as likely to take the place of coffee or chicory.

Every package must be of one-quarter of a pound and bear a movable stamp indicating the nature and proportions of the contents. All violations of this regulation are visited with confiscation of the article and a fine of twenty pounds, and any one using stamps already employed is subject to a fine of one hundred pounds. Pure coffee and chicory are not subject to this regulation, but a mixture of the two must bear the lawful stamp.

In this way imitations of coffee cannot be sold without the knowledge of the buyer, and are subject to a heavier tax than the genuine coffee and chicory.

II.

COFFEE FROM AN ECONOMIC STANDPOINT.

SUMMARY :—*Increase of growth and consumption.*—*Accidental decline in prices.*—*Consumption of coffee.*—*Average consumption per head.*—*Duties on the importation of coffee.*—*The 'duty of societies against the abuse of alcoholic drinks to be the first to demand a diminution of import duties on coffee.*

In order to form an opinion in regard to the future of this product, one must take into consideration the history of its production and consumption. Up to this time the statistics seem to indicate that the consumption is increasing more rapidly than the production, in spite of appearances to the contrary. Thus, from 1855 to 1878, the general production has increased 48% and the consumption 60%, the balance being, as is seen, in favor of the consumption. If, then, the consumption has gained 12% over the production, how shall we explain the decline in the price of 40% in two years ? We must look for the solution of the problem in another direction.

It is not the equilibrium between production and consumption that is broken, but between supply and demand, which is a different thing. They have changed without an appreciable transition, in Brazil, from the transportation on the backs of mules to that by locomotive. The crops reach us, therefore, at least two months sooner than formerly, and in twenty-two days are transported by steamers to the markets of consumption, which was formerly accomplished by sailing vessels in eighty days. Here is, in all, a gain of four months, and consequently one-third of the crop offered to consumers before half the preceding one has been exhausted. The demand does not increase in the same ratio as the rapidity of the supply. The question of production does not enter here ; and even if Brazil had not increased its production by a single bag, the same phenomena would have appeared.

With respect to the crops of India, the reasoning is still more applicable ; for the sailing vessels doubling Cape Good Hope and the steamships passing through the Suez Canal, deposit in the warehouses of Europe two crops with a very brief interval, so that, owing to the *rapidity of arrivals*, for every one demand there are *two* others.

To these grand causes, must be added, in the case of Brazil, others of a secondary importance, for example : the great crop of 1880, the unwise distribution of shipments from the interior, the planters sending sometimes more than 30,000 bags per day, whereas had their shipments been distributed more evenly throughout the year not more than one-half this amount would have been reached ; then the extravagances of the telegrams, offering coffee below the market to obtain orders, etc.

For arriving at the conclusion that there has been a great increase in production, the large stocks and particularly the enormous one at Havre, are taken as a basis of estimation. This is an error, since the accumulation of stocks in the sea-ports is only the consequence of the increased facilities for transportation throughout the world. We are, then, in face of a transitory situation due to *new means of transportation*.

But the shock is over and cannot be repeated until means of transportation have been found as much superior to the present as they are to those formerly employed. Such being the case, with the same facilities for transportation, the difference between the supply and demand must necessarily diminish, since it is really *the consumption which is increasing.*

---

* See Dr. Meplain, *Du Café, étude de Thérapeutique Physiologique*, Paris. 1868, Louis Leclerc, Libraire-Editeur; Dr. Guégan, Considérations sur l'Emploi du Café dans le traitement des métrorrhagies, Paris, 1881, A. Parent, Imprimeur de la Faculté de Médecine ; Dr. Villemus, *Du Café et de ses principales applications thérapeutiques*, Paris, 1875, A. Derenne; Dr. C. Teixeira, *Der Kaffee*, Vienna, 1883 ; Dr. Cunha e Souza, *Brasil-Kaffee*, Vienna, 1884 ; Baron de Theresopolis, *Discours au 4e Congrès International d' Hygiène et de Démographie à Genève* (1882).

The production of the entire world may be stated as follows :

95,000,000 kilogrammes in 1832.
300,000,000   "   " 1855.
600,000,000   "   " 1880.

Up to 1878 the price of coffee was constantly increasing.

The coffee of Brazil, while advancing with the rest, was always quoted from 15 to 20 francs below those of other countries.

This inferiority in price, due to more economical methods of production, has created a demand in France for Brazilian coffee, where it has been sold under the names of Reunion, Martinique, Zanzibar, etc. Since 1879, Brazilian coffees have continued to decline in price.

The 4,337,418 bags of Rio coffee exported in 1881, which, at the average price of the preceding year, would have represented the sum of $60,000,000, have produced, at the mean price of 1881, only $47,000,000 ; that is, the return has been diminished 21.4 per cent. Santos exported, in 1880-81, 1,204,198 bags.

On the other hand, although the consumption of coffee has continued to increase while the prices were declining, the retail trade has shown great timidity, never venturing to keep on hand more than the quantity necessary for its current demands ; and in this it has been encouraged by the course of prices during the last few years ; so that it is not at all astonishing that large stocks have accumulated at the sea-ports, while very little remains in the hands of the retail trade.

But there are limits at last to everything, and it is not to be supposed that so important and necessary an article as coffee can decline to a ridiculous price, though for the moment it may suffer some discredit.

It is established by official and authentic statistics :

1. That the production of Brazilian coffee has been constantly on the increase.
2. That the consumption of coffee in foreign countries has been continually extending.
3. That since 1879-80 the price of Brazilian coffee has gone on steadily diminishing.

To what cause shall this enormous and obstinate divergence be attributed ? Have the coffees of Brazil suffered from foreign competition ? This does not appear from the statistics of exportation. On the contrary, the coffees of Santos and S. Paulo are constantly supplanting those of S. Domingo ; and alone the stock of Brazilian coffee is greater than all receipts from other countries. The reason for the decline must be sought for, then, elsewhere, and it is unquestionably to be found in the fact *that the demand is less than the amount put on the market.* The equilibrium between consumption and production no longer exists. There seems to be only one remedy for this difficulty : *to open new markets and lessen the duties on imports.*

It is to be hoped that the various governments will understand at last all the advantages that would result for the public health and well-being, from the suppression of the duties on an article so necessary as coffee.

The excessive production and the too rapid extension of coffee culture, to the detriment of the existing plantations in South America, must also be added to the causes of the present critical situation. But the remedy for this must not be looked for in a diminution of this culture, but in the removal of all the obstacles which stand in the way of the opening of new markets or enlarging the old ones.

Since in an average year Europe and America consume about 600,000,000 kilogrammes of coffee, and inasmuch as these countries might consume three or four times this amount, it appears to us more logical and more advantageous rather *to extend the market than to restrict the production.*

Statistics show that the consumption of coffee in a given country is in the inverse ratio of import duties ; that is, the higher the duties on its importation, the less is its consumption in that country.

Let the figures speak for us ; and let us first consider those of 1879.

Considering the consumption of coffee by countries, we find that the greater per capita consumption is in Holland, where it amounts to 8 kilogrammes, 12 grammes to each inhabitant ; and in that country there is no duty on coffee.

In Belgium, where the duty is only 13 francs, 20 centimes per 100 kilogrammes, the consumption per head is 5 kilogrammes, 400 grammes.

In the United States, where coffee pays no duty, and in Switzerland, where it is taxed only 3 francs per 100 kilogrammes, the consumption is, respectively, 3 kilogrammes, 500 grammes, and 3 kilogrammes, 600 grammes, per head.

After these countries the consumption diminishes, and in Germany, where the duty is 50 francs per 100 kilogrammes, the per capita consumption is only 2 kilogrammes, 470 grammes.

In Austria the duty is 16 florins gold per 100 kilogrammes and the consumption 1 kilogramme, 50 grammes.

In France, thanks to the duty, almost prohibitory, of 156 francs per 100 kilogrammes, the consumption per head is only 1 kilogramme, 460 grammes. The Frenchman, then, consumes only one-sixth as much as the Dutchman and one-fourth as much as the Belgian.

The Switzer or the inhabitant of the United States uses thrice as much as the Frenchman, and the German twice as much.

Societies for the suppression of the abuse of alcoholic liquors can do no better work than in demanding a reduction in the duties which weigh so heavily on coffee in France and elsewhere. The show cases of the shops do not contain a single sample of the coffee of Brazil, in spite of the fact that that country alone exports more than all others together.

The world's total production in 1878 was estimated at 491,000,000 kilogrammes, and that of Brazil alone was more than 250,000,000.[*]

---

[*] We have already remarked that the total annual production at this time is 666,000,000 kilogrammes, of which 360,000,000 are produced by Brazil against 306,000,000 by all the other countries together.

A DISCOURSE ON BRAZILIAN COFFEE,

BASED UPON ANALYSES MADE BY

PROF. ERNST LUDWIG IN VIENNA,

PRONOUNCED BY

Doctor C. TEIXEIRA,

VIENNA, 1883.

A DISCOURSE ON BRAZILIAN COFFEE.

I.—*Liebig's opinion.—Coffee as an excitant of cerebral activity.—Discovery of caffeine.—Coffee as a source of nutrition: Marvaud's opinion.--Experiments of Stuhlmann, Falck and Leven.—Opinion of Schultz.—Gasparin.—Effects of coffee upon the bodily exchanges of matter: experiments of Böcker, Lehmann, and Marvaud.—Color of the coffee bean: its size, weight and age.*

If it be desired to discuss any given kind of coffee, one must consider the wants and preference to be met by them in comparison with other sorts, in order to set them in their true light ; and in this, as in every other genuine discussion, the best criteria are necessary. These criteria can only be reached by a thorough understanding of the point in view, from which the coffee is to be considered, whether in respect to its properties or otherwise.

It appears therefore necessary, before approaching the real task which we have undertaken, namely, the discussion of Brazilian coffee, to set forth what has been decided in regard to it by scientific researches.

"It will always remain a mystery," says Liebig, in his work "Organic Chemistry in its Application to Physiology and Pathology," "how men first conceived the idea of making a beverage by pouring hot water on the leaves of a certain shrub or by boiling the seeds roasted ; but there must have been a cause why it (coffee) has become a necessity of life to whole nations." Science, indeed, has ascertained this cause and has shown that these artificial beverages are not only agreeable, but also satisfy real wants of the organism, agreeably exciting our minds and activities, as well as our powers of endurance ; while, on the other hand, absence from them is attended by a lowering of the nutritive functions.

To coffee has justly been assigned the first place as an excitant of cerebral activity ; and it is, indeed, the beverage of the intelligence. By its influence upon the brain its functions are quickened, its receptibility to the impressions afforded by the senses is heightened, the progenitive proclivity is awakened, and thought and imagination quickened and intensified ; and this without disturbing the quiet of the judgment, or confusing the logical sequence of the ideas. On the contrary, while the imagination is enlivened, the mental impressions are deepened, and while intensity and clearness are added to thought, the powers of judgment are raised to the highest degree. While coffee shares with alcohol the property of exciting the brain, it must be preferred to the latter in regard to the ulterior effects.

What makes coffee more valuable in this regard is that it does not fatigue the nerves ; that it does not, like alcoholic beverages, produce confusion, and that the excitement produced by it does not leave that depression which follows alcoholic stimulation. To produce its effects to the full extent the beans must pass through the process of roasting ; for it has been ascertained by experiment that the infusions of the green beans do not produce that excitation and heightening of the brain functions in so high a degree as those of roasted beans. This valuable effect of coffee is not, then, to be ascribed alone to the natural components of the coffee bean, but principally to substances developed in the process of roasting.

It is accepted by most chemists that the essential oil of coffee, a volatile oil, of the composition $C_8H_{10}O_2$, is the source of the stimulant effects of coffee ; but caffeine has, doubtless, its share in producing this effect ; and as this substance is the principal factor of the value of coffee, as a conservative agent, we will now devote a short space to its consideration.

Caffeine is an alkaloid—that is, one of the vegetable organic bodies, of the composition $C_8H_{10}N_4O_2$. It was discovered in coffee in the year 1820 by Runge, and analyzed by Pelletier and Robiquet in 1821. It forms white, silky, shining crystals, is slightly bitter in taste, is soluble in water, alcohol and chloroform, and less readily in ether. Vaporized with chlorine, it leaves a brown trace, which, when exposed to ammonia, takes a purple-violet color. It is employed in medicine on account of its energetic influence on the nerve centers.

Liebig, in his valuation of coffee as a source of nutrition, attributes the chief influence to the leading part occupied by caffeine as a constituent of taurine in the gall, it being composed as follows :

1 Atom Caffeine,	- - - - - -	$C_8 H_{10} N_4 O_2$
9 Atom Water,	- - - - - -	$(H_2 O_9)$
9 Atom Oxygen,	- - - - -	O_9

When, however, Marvaud, in a valuable work, "Des Aliments d'Epargne," declares that Liebig represents coffee merely as a stimulant which is supposed to excite the secretions of the gall, he is greatly in error. The role attributed by Liebig to coffee and tea in regard to their nutritious properties is of far more importance, for he expressly says, " It cannot be denied that through an excess of nitrogenous substances or the want of exercise, on which depend the internal processes of waste and nutrition, it produces the nitrogenous compositions necessary to the formation of gall ; that in this condition the appropriation of nutritious substances is defective, which deficiency it is the business of the matter produced by respiration to supply."

In Liebig's opinion, the function of caffeine does not, as Marvaud represents, consist entirely in assisting the secretion of gall, but in supplying to some extent the want of nitrogen in cases of insufficiency of food, while after being converted into taurine it assists the functions of respiration, or rather makes up for the deficiencies in that respect.

This opinion of Liebig, however, which was based on theoretical deductions, did not support the test of experimental criticism, and is now considered untenable. It is a fact that coffee affects the digestive functions also.

Stuhlmann, Falck and Loven established by experiments that caffeine especially excites a more energetic action of the salivary glands, and also stimulates the muscular contractions of the stomach and intestines, and that taken in inordinate doses it produces cramp-like pains and their attendant contractions. It would, however, be an error to confine the whole of the effects of coffee to this action, for caffeine, beyond a doubt, plays in the human organism a much more important role.

As long ago as 1831, the physiologist Schultz, at Berlin, declared that coffee as well as alcoholic spirits, possesses a decided influence on the internal processes of nutrition ; that while furnishing little nutritious matters of themselves, they prevent, to a certain extent, the demand for them. Schultz was the first who applied to these substances the term "Aliments d'Epargne." The theory of these "Aliments d'Epargne" has been supported by so many scientific experiments and so substantiated by experience, that it may be accepted as correct, though it has its opponents.

Physiologists teach us that an adult, in order to preserve the even balance of his bodily functions, when performing a moderate amount of physical labor, requires 20.7 grammes of nitrogen daily, and with severer labor 25.9 grammes. If, however, an analysis be made of the ordinary food of the poor and laboring population of the great manufacturing towns, it will be found that the daily amount of nitrogen consumed is considerably less than the minimum given by physiologists, without injury to the health or a diminution of capacity for work.

In all these cases we find, however, that relatively large quantities of alcoholic stimulants, or coffee or tea, are taken. Gasparin has observed that for the miners of Charleroi, 15 grammes daily of nitrogen was sufficient, as shown by the following exhibit of their daily food :

2 Liters Coffee,	30.59 grammes, furnishing	0.222 grammes nitrogen		
Chicory,	30.59 "	"	0.176	" "
¼ Liter Milk,	- - - - -	0.114	" "	
1 Kilogramme Bread,	- - - -	12.500	" "	
Butter	60.00 grammes, - -	0.004	" "	
Vegetables,	750.00 " -	0.037	" "	
Meat,	75.00 " -	1.767	" "	
	Total, -	14.820	" "	

This food is less nourishing than that of the Trappists, who are, as is well known, compelled to an extreme of bodily mortification by the rules of their order ; for, according to Gasparin, their average daily consumption of nitrogen is 15 grammes. If it be asked how these miners of Charleroi are enabled to maintain their bodily vigor with a quantity of food so apparently insufficient, and at hard labor, we can only reply that such a result must be attributed to the coffee. Physiologists employ as a scale for determining the intensity with which the exchange of matter in the body proceeds, the quantity of urea and uric acid which are secreted in a given time. In order, now, to prove scientifically the effects of coffee upon the bodily exchanges of matter, Böcker and Lehmann, and after them, several others, have made many experiments with that view upon healthy persons, and have determined the amounts of urea and uric acid which will be secreted during 24 hours, when, with the usual diet, no coffee is taken, and when, on the other hand, coffee is constantly taken. We extract from the work of Böcker the following table :

Quantity of urine	in 24 hours, without coffee,	1364 5	cu. cen.		
"	" "	with	"	1739.75	
"	urea	"	without	"	22.275 grammes
"	"	"	with	"	12.585 "
"	uric acid	"	without	"	0.587 "
"	"	"	with	"	0.402 "

Experiments made by Prof. Angel Marvaud, in 1861, gave the following results :

Without coffee, quantity of urine		discharged,	1531 cu. cen.		
"	"	"	urea		38.44 grammes.
"	"	"	uric acid	"	.40 "
"	"	solid matter in urine,		- -	53.84 "
With	coffee, quantity of urine,	-	-	1395	cu. cen.
"	"	"	urea,	-	33.14 grammes.
"	"	"	uric acid,	- -	.22 "
"	"	solid matters,		- -	46.05 "

These figures, whose reliability is attested by the reputation of these experimenters, show in the clearest manner, that coffee influences the quantity of nitrogenous urinal matter secreted, and at the same time the intensity of the urinal secretions. While lowering the rate of decomposition and assimilation, operating as a brake on molecular changes, it certainly lessens the amount of nutrition needed by the system. Examination and experiment have further shown the results and beneficial effects of coffee already shown to be due to the presence of caffeine. If it be, then, the question to determine the value of any coffee as an "Aliment d'Epargne," we must adopt as the criterion of our decision the relative amount of its caffeine. Whatever the influence to be attributed to the other chemical components of the coffee, the nutritious properties of the albumen, fatty substances and sugar, which constitute the chief part of them, are so generally known that we think it unnecessary to discuss them here. We only wish to state that, in our determination of the value of a coffee, it is necessary to take into account its relative amount of these substances. It appears, then, from these considerations, that it is the quantitative chemical analysis which furnishes the rational scientific basis for the determination of the value of a given amount of coffee.

The appearance, shape, size and color of the beans vary greatly, depending, not only upon the cultivation, but upon the conditions of greater or less maturity in which the fruit has been gathered ; so that it would be difficult to judge correctly from these indications alone. The color, particularly, exhibits all possible gradations of yellow, yellowish, brown-yellow, yellow-brown, to brown, black-brown, green, yellowish and bluish-green. In general the preference is to be given to the light-colored kinds ; the much esteemed green being either an indication that the fruit has been gathered in an unripe condition, or that the beans have been artificially colored, as is often practiced, and by coloring matters injurious to health.

A bean of large size and uniform shape is justly to be preferred, as these conditions show complete maturity, careful handling and selection. The worst sorts are the uneven, unclean and high-colored. A most valuable physical property of coffee is its density. As coffee is generally bought and sold by weight, neither buyer nor seller can be indifferent to a possible variation of 600 to 700 grammes per deciliter.

The advantage of the seller would be served by having a heavier sort, while the interest of the buyer consists in getting a lighter kind, since in this case he obtains a greater quantity for a given weight ; but also, for a more important reason must the consumer prefer a lighter sort, viz., that coffee, like wine, gains in delicacy of aroma the longer the period between the gathering and the use.

With increasing age the beans become considerably lighter, so that the specific weight becomes a factor in the estimation of the value of any coffee.

II.—*History of coffee culture.—Introduction of coffee in Europe.—Coffee in America.—Brazil produces half of the coffee of the world.—Increase of this production.—Prof. Ernst Ludwig's analysis of Brazilian coffee.—Brazilian coffee contains more nutritious properties than other coffees.—Aubert's and Payen's studies.—Table of weight of different coffees shows that Brazilian coffee ranks with the best.*

Although in its home, Caffa, from which it derives its name, the use of coffee has long been known, it was only in the beginning of the 15th century that it began to extend beyond the frontiers of this district and that it began to be planted in Yemen.

A Mufti, Gemel Eddin, a native of Aden, in one of his travels, became acquainted with coffee, and, on his return, introduced its use among the Dervishes, as a means of arousing their wakefulness and recollection of the hours of prayer. Its use extended, in a short time, throughout Arabia. In the year 1511 the Pasha Kheir Bey instituted the first crusade against it, forbidding its sale and destroying the plantations ; but his successor, recognizing its agreeable effects, assisted in its dissemination. We learn from the Arabian literature of the 16th century, which contains as many panegyrics as invectives in regard to its effects, what continual strife has attended its spread.

We first hear of coffee in Europe from Ranwolf, who made its acquaintance in Aleppo, and the first botanical description was given by Prosper Alpinus, in 1582. In 1624, the Venetians brought a great quantity of it to Europe, and in 1645 it was in general use in Southern Italy.

Coffee was made known to the court of Louis XIV by an ambassador of Mohammed IV, and in 1670 the first coffee-house was opened at Marseilles. In 1652 coffee made its first appearance in England, and in Germany in 1670. The first coffee-house was established at Vienna in 1683, and at Berlin in 1711. Frederick II created a state establishment for coffee roasting, at which one was forced to pay six times the price paid to private dealers. He made the trade in coffee a royal monopoly, and it was permitted only to the nobility, the clergy and the higher officials, to roast coffee for themselves. He discouraged its use among the lower classes, as he did not wish the money necessary to its purchase to leave the country.

Towards the close of the last century, coffee was in use at all the German courts and also in many private houses ; but it was always a luxury for the rich alone, owing to its high price.

In 1650, the Dutch had brought some little coffee plants to Bourbon, and, as they flourished well, large plantations were commenced towards the close of the 17th century. In 1726 a small plant stock was carried to Martinique, whence, in a short time, the cultivation spread to San Domingo, Guadalupe and Cayenne. Before the French Revolution, San Domingo, Martinique and Bourbon sent to Europe the greater part of its coffee ; but when the plantations in San Domingo were destroyed by the negro insurrections, the cultivation of coffee emigrated to Ceylon, Java, Cuba and Venezuela.

In the first part of the present century, the islands of Ceylon, Java, and Sumatra provided Europe with its coffee. At the present time the greater part of the coffee consumed in Europe comes from Brazil, whose coffee production is equal to that of all the rest of the world. During the last ten years the following quantities of coffee have been exported from the various countries :

French Possessions in Africa and West Indies, -					16,995 Cwt.
Menado,	-	-	-	-	18,450 "
Moka,	-	-	-	-	19,054 "
Cuba,	-	-	-	-	24,000 "
S. Salvador,	-	-	-	-	92,000 "
Colombia,	-	-	-	-	98,204 "
Guatemala,	-	-	-	-	120,716 "
Costa Rica,	-	-	-	-	185,472 "
Porto Rico,	-	-	-	-	192,645 "
Venezuela,	-	-	-	-	230,000 "
East Indies,	-	-	-	-	412,000 "
S. Domingo, -			-	-	606,000 "
Ceylon, -	-	-	-	-	850,000 "
Java and Sumatra, -			-	-	1,415,105 "
		Total,	-	-	4,280,641 Cwt.
Brazil,	-	-	-	-	4,250,000 "

The coffee culture of Brazil, which at the present time, is the chief source of the wealth of that immense Empire, so favored by nature, has risen, in a remarkably short time, from very small beginnings to its present extent. In the year 1723, the first coffee plant was brought from Cayenne to Brazil ; but the experiment of its cultivation was a failure in the Province of Para, the soil and climate of this Province proving unsuitable to it. Fifty years later, however, a Franciscan monk succeeded in establishing a small plantation in the Province of Rio de Janeiro, and from this the culture extended into the adjoining country. At the present time, in the four most important Provinces of Brazil, Rio de Janeiro, S. Paulo, Minas Geraes, and Espirito Santo, an extent of several million square metres is exclusively devoted to the cultivation of coffee. Nearly all the soil which can be reclaimed from the forests is planted with coffee plants. The trees and bushes are burned to the ground, their ashes affording to the soil the organic matters which are required by the coffee plant. Nine hundred and eighteen plants to the hectare can be set, which will produce an average of 2,000 kilogrammes annually.

Although one must wait from four to six years for the first crop, and the young plants require constant and careful attention, the time and labor are well rewarded by the subsequent product, as is proved by the extraordinary increase in its culture.

With what astonishing rapidity the coffee culture of Brazil has increased, may be seen from the following data :

Exports in the year 1877,	-	-	170,793.300	Kilogrammes.
"	"	1878,	-	-	181,871.840	"
"	"	1879,	-	-	212,110.980	"
"	"	1880,	-	-	213,783.240	"
"	"	1881,	-	-	262,645.080	"

In the period from 1877 to 1881 there were exported 1,041,204.440 kilogrammes ; from 1868 to 1874, 165,114.223 kilogrammes ; and from 1838 to 1844, only 83,687.846 kilogrammes.

A glance at this table is sufficient to see with what rapidity coffee culture in Brazil has increased from year to year, and what an enormous quantity that country furnishes for the world's consumption. If the production of Brazilian coffee should continue to increase at a like rate, as it may be reasonably expected to do, the time must come when it will drive all other kinds from the markets of the world, or at least will take the principal place. That its real value entitles it to occupy this place will be proved by reliable statistics from scientific experiments and comparisons.

Led by the conviction that for a rational estimate of the value of any kind of coffee, there is necessary, above all, a carefully conducted qualitative and quantitative analysis, the author of this discourse requested Prof. Ernst Ludwig, Director of the Chemical Institute of the Medical Faculty of the University of Vienna, to subject to an analysis two kinds of Brazilian coffee, both from the same plantation, viz., the Plantation of Cachoeira, belonging to Dr. Lazzarini, and only differing in age. Prof. Ludwig was kind enough to analyze the two kinds, employing the method laid down by Dragendorff. The analysis gave the following results :

WASHED COFFEE.

	The Newer.	The Older.
Water, - - -	11.65 %	12.07 %
Ashes CO_2,	3.55 "	3.75 "
Tannic Acid, -	5.84 "	7.01 "
Caffeine, - - -	**1.16** "	**1.75** "
Fats, - - -	14.10 "	14.06 "
Sugar, - - -	5.96 "	6.36 "
Albumen, - - -	13.92 "	12.19 "
Cellulose, Pectin, Extractive matter, -	43.82 "	42.81 "
	100.00 %	100.00 %

One hundred parts of the ashes contain :

SOLUBLE PARTS.

	Newer.	Older.
Potash, -	49.57 %	49.38 %
Soda, - - -	0.73 "	0.71 "
Magnesia, - - -	0.06 "	0.08 "
Chlorine, - - -	0.39 "	0.54 "
Phosphor. Anhyd.,	0.09 "	0.15 "
Sulph. "	5.37 "	4.08 "
Carbon "	20.55 "	20.65 "
	76.76 %	76.69 %

INSOLUBLE PARTS.

	Newer.	Older.
Lime, - - -	2.86 %	3.34%
Magnesia, - - -	7.93 "	7.77 "
Oxide of Iron, -	0.17 "	0.03 "
Phos. Anhyd.,	6.91 "	5.36 "
Carb. " -	4.54 "	5.97 "
Sulph. "	0.16 "	0.28 "
Silicic Acid, -	0.67 "	0.56 "
	23.24 %	23.31 %
Total, -	100.00 %	100.00 %

(Signed) IMPERIAL INSTITUTE OF PATHOLOGICAL CHEMISTRY,

E. LUDWIG, M. P.

As is shown in the above analysis, the most important substances are those possessing nutritious properties, notably the caffeine, which, in the Brazilian product, constitutes from 1.16% to 1.75% : and the following comparative table made from the results obtained by other chemists, shows that with respect to the amount of caffeine contained, no other kind can equal the Brazilian coffee, much less excel it :

NAME OF CHEMIST.	KIND OF COFFEE.	AMOUNT OF CAFFEINE.
Graham, Stenhouse and Campbell.	Wild Ceylon	0.87 %
" " "	Plantation Ceylon	0.54—0.83 "
Robiquet and Boutron	Martinique	0.36 "
" " "	Alexandria	0.24 "
" " "	Java	0.25 "
" " "	Moka	0.21 "
" " "	Cayenne	0.20 "
" " "	S. Domingo	0.17 "
Döbereiner	Moka	0.60 "
Vasman	"	0.5—0.7 "
Pucetti	"	0.4 "
Aubert	Java	0.709—0.849 "
Ludwig	Brazilian	1.16—1.75 "

Of the numbers exhibited by this table, the most important for our purpose are those found by Aubert, in Rostock, as this experimenter experimented on the one hand with one of the best kinds of coffee, and, on the other, made use of a method to which no exceptions can be taken, as giving too small quantities.

Aubert's method is based on the readiness with which caffeine dissolves in chloroform, particularly if the latter be hot, and on the insolubility of the other constituents in the same liquid. Some coffee was filtered and evaporated at 100° Celsius to the consistence of syrup, the residue put into a glass and about the same volume of chloroform poured on it. The glass, having been covered, was left standing one day in a bath at a temperature a little less than 68°, the contents being agitated from time to time. The chloroform was then poured off and evaporated. The filtration was continued with the grounds of the coffee until no caffeine was taken up by the chloroform. There remained from the evaporation of the chloroform a brown substance, from which, by treating it with cold ether, a brown matter of agreeable odor was extracted, and a fat. Caffeine is but slightly soluble in ether, about one part in 1,000 of ether. After the evaporation of the ether, a little caffeine is left. crystallized in fine needles, which, after washing in ether, can be kept quite pure. The brown matter deposited by the ether can be formed into silky filaments by successive solutions in chloroform and water, and evaporated to dryness. In this manner Aubert ascertained the quantity of caffeine in some excellent specimens of Java coffee to be from 0.709% to 0.840%.

Comparing these figures with those obtained by the equally faultless method of Ludwig, viz., 1.16% to 1.75%, the superiority of the Brazilian coffee is clearly seen ; there being in favor of the latter a difference of 0.451% to 0.901%.

Of the remaining chemical constituents of coffee of nutritious value, there are now to be considered the fats, the albuminoids, and the sugar.

The analysis of Prof. Ludwig further shows that Brazilian coffee contains 14.06% to 14.10% of fat, 12.19% to 13.92% of albuminoids, and 5.96% to 6.36% of sugar.

According to the experiments of Payen, the eminent French chemist, who analyzed various kinds of coffee, a good kind should contain 10% to 13% of fat, and 10% of albuminoids. The proportion of sugar he has not clearly determined, but simply says that sugar, dextrine, acids and an uncertain vegetable substance, are together found to the amount of 15 5%. A comparison of- the special results of Ludwig with the general remarks of Payen, shows, then, that Brazilian coffee, even in respect to the fat and albuminoids, is of the highest value, easily satisfying the most exacting demands. The analyses of Prof. Ludwig give, also, a scientific confirmation to the results of general experience that coffee increases in value with increasing age ; the two analyses of coffees coming from the same plantation, and differing in age alone, exhibiting remarkable differences in chemical constitution. The quantities of albuminoids and fats are greater in the newer sample, while the tannic acid, the sugar and the caffeine exist in a greater proportion in the older. Since caffeine is the most important constituent, it follows that preference must be given to the older, as containing the greater quantity of that alkaloid.

It is, however, to be well understood that this is the case only when the coffee is properly kept. The appearance alone of coffee, as has been already remarked, does not afford reliable means of forming a judgment of its value ; but the flavor and aroma are not to be disregarded, though matters of personal or local preference affording an application of the proverb "chacun a son goût."

It is altogether probable that in these respects the coffee of Brazil is not inferior to the other kinds, an evidence of which is its immense consumption in Europe. A comparison by weight, as shown in the following table, proves that Brazilian coffee ranks with the best :

COUNTRY.	YEAR OF GATHERING.	WEIGHT PER DECILITER.	No. OF BEANS PER DECILITER.
Moka, - - -	1828	500 Grammes	510
Zanzibar, -	1874	606 "	554
Java, - - -	1874	455 "	338
Ceylon, -	1872	508 "	345
Reunion.	1869	630 "	488
Venezuela, - -	1865	654 "	400
Guadalupe, -	1875	660 "	382
Martinique, -	1873	630 "	414
Hayti, - - -	1874	642 "	358
Espirito Santo (Brazil), -	1875	567 "	318
Rio de Janeiro, " -	1872	522 "	294

III. — *Why Brazilian coffee is little known in Europe as such.—Foreign denominations given to it, and only the inferior sorts sold as Brazilian.—Admixtures.—Work of the Association Centro da Lavoura e Commercio of Rio de Janeiro.—Its exhibitions.—Prices.*

It is shown by official statistics that the greater part of the coffee consumed in Europe comes from Brazil; and using the results of scientific experiments, we have established that it deserves to be regarded as of the best kind.

In face of these indisputable facts, every one will be astonished to learn that so little is known of the coffee of Brazil as such, and that the majority of its consumers do not even know that it comes from Brazil. The reason for these astonishing facts are the following:

In the first place, we must point out that, until the middle of the present century, the coffee-planters of Brazil did not take sufficient care, nor had sufficient knowledge to obtain the best products, and consequently Brazilian coffee was for a long period really inferior to the kinds of other countries, but little esteemed and commanding a low price. In the course of time, however, the production has not only enormously increased, but the quality has been greatly improved, until at present, as we have shown, no coffee in the world excels in intrinsic value the good Brazilian grades, and but few can be compared with them. Up to the present, this important fact is known only to the producer and the dealer; the consuming public, even the best informed, not knowing that the best coffee in the markets comes from Brazil. The cause of this is the handling of the intermediaries, through whose hands it passes in going from the producer to the consumer. The planter consigns his coffee to a commission merchant, and from him it goes into the hands of the sacker, who assorts it, habitually mixing the better with the poorer sorts. It is next bought by the exporter, in quantities of from 500 to 5,000 sacks, and shipped *en masse* to Hamburg, Bordeaux, Havre, Marseilles, Liverpool, etc. Here a commission merchant sells it by wholesale to the speculator, who subjects it to all the manipulations from which he expects an advantage to his pockets.

He assorts it again; gives to the better sorts the names of "Superior Moka," "Java," "Ceylon," and introduces them under these names into the market. Only the inferior sorts, the refuse, are sold as native Brazilian coffee; and even these are still further deteriorated by the admixture of the poorest Costa Rica and Venezuela coffee. In this way the speculator secures a double gain; since he lessens the demand for Brazilian coffee as such, thus compelling the planter to sell his crop for low prices, and, on the other hand, selling the greater part of his cheap purchases for the best possible price. The indifference of the planter who, even at a low price, reaps large profits from his coffee plantations, has made these manipulations of the speculators quite easy.

In view of these, it is easily understood that, in spite of the enormous quantity of the coffee of Brazil imported into Europe, and despite its excellent qualities, so little should be heard of it. As a matter of fact, the greater part of that coffee planted, gathered, and sold in Brazil, and which we so much enjoy and buy so dearly as Moka or Ceylon, has been rebaptized by the speculators of Hamburg, Bordeaux, etc., with a false name and sold at a large profit.

To prevent these operations of the speculators, a general knowledge of the whole subject must be possessed by the consuming public. It was only recently that the planters of Brazil arrived at this conclusion; and they have formed a society which has for its object the opening of exhibitions of the coffee of Brazil in the principal European cities, so that the opportunity may be afforded to all to convince themselves of its superior qualities, and to compare it with that which is sold by dealers under the name of Brazilian coffee.

In several cities these exhibitions have been already held, and the products there exhibited have excited general admiration; but the operations of the speculators would be more effectually checked by diminishing the number of middlemen, through whose hands the coffee must now pass, between the grower and the consumer. How much cheaper coffee would become to the consumer may be seen by comparing the price at which the planter sells his product with that paid by the consumer to the dealer. In the last two years the planters have received from the exporters the following prices:

1880.

FIRST SIX MONTHS. PER KILOGRAMME.		SECOND SIX MONTHS. PER KILOGRAMME.	
First good,	56—63 kreutzers.	45—60 kreutzers.	
" regular,	52—60 "	42—57 "	
" ordinary,	49—58 "	37—52 "	
Second good,	44—53 "	35—47 "	
" ordinary,	39—47 "	30—41 "	

1881.

FIRST SIX MONTHS. PER KILOGRAMME.		SECOND SIX MONTHS. PER KILOGRAMME.	
First good,	43—50 kreutzers.	41—50 kreutzers.	
" regular,	39—47 "	37—46 "	
" ordinary,	33—43 "	33—40 "	
Second good,	27—38 "	28—33 "	
" ordinary,	23—33 "	24—29 "	

IV. — *The abuse of alcoholic beverages.—Alcoholism checked by the use of coffee.—Great benefit to Nations.—Consumption of coffee per capita for the year 1879.—Conclusion.*

The fearful consequences produced by the abuse of alcoholic beverages are generally known; how it enfeebles the vital organs, reduces the power of resistance, finally effecting a general degradation of mind and body. It would, however, be wrong to attribute the poverty and misery of the lower classes to the constantly increasing consumption of alcohol alone. The abuse of alcoholic drinks is rather the consequence than the cause of this misery.

That a well-fed man, living in easy circumstances, should give himself up to the abuse of alcoholic liquors, should be regarded as an exceptional case; but the laborer who gains by his bodily labor less than his necessities demand for his nourishment and sustenance, feels himself impelled as if by a necessity to lay hold on the bottle. Alcohol excites his nervous system, restores his tired limbs, and enables him to accomplish his work on relatively less nourishment.

If the poor laborer would confine himself to taking only the small quantity needed to accomplish the above results, alcohol might then be regarded as the true elixir of life for the poor. Unfortunately, the case is quite different; as only in a few cases, as is well known, does the drinker of alcohol take only the small amount needed to maintain his forces, prizing most the exhilarating effects which remove from him the cold reality and replace it with happy delusions. He becomes a confirmed drinker, ruins his health and brings sorrow to all his belongings. Thus poverty leads to the abuse of alcohol, the consequence of which is misery. Each is a corollary of the other.

It is a duty binding on humanity to oppose the steadily increasing and so destructive consequences of alcoholism ; and this can be done in two ways, either by bettering the condition of the laborer, thus removing the cause, or by the general introduction of a substance whose use produces the beneficial effects of moderate doses of alcohol, and not, like that, produces injurious results, even when used in excess, and does not invite immoderation. Such a substance, above all others, is coffee, of great service as a stimulant, not conducing to excess, whose effects are beneficial only and incapable of doing injury.

It is proved that in all countries where the working class is possessed of a certain degree of intelligence, the use of alcohol has been gradually replaced by that of coffee. Every step in this direction may be regarded as in the interest of humanity, and it is to be regretted that the governments of many States have placed so high duties upon the importation of coffee, thus raising the price and making the enjoyment of this valuable stimulant almost an impossibility to the poor.

Statistics show the truth of that which was *a priori* to be expected, that the consumption of coffee in any given country stands in inverse ratio to the rate of duty levied upon its importation, that the higher the duty the less the consumption per capita each year.

In the following countries the per capita consumption of coffee for the year 1879 was as follows :

COUNTRY.	TAX PER 100 KILOGRAMMES.	CONSUMPTION PER CAPITA.
Germany	50 francs	2.47 Kilogrammes.
Austria	16 gold florins	1.05 "
France	150 francs	1.46 "
Belgium	13.20 francs	5.40 "
Holland	None	8.12 "
Switzerland	3 francs	3.60 "
United States	None	3.50 "

In order, then, that coffee may accomplish its good work of supplanting alcohol, it is necessary either that duties should be considerably reduced, or abolished altogether ; but it is also necessary that Brazilian coffee, which, as has been shown, combines the highest qualities with a low price, should reach the consumer in the shortest way, unmixed and under its honest name.

Brazilian Coffee.

Opinions of Scientists on its Merit.

BRAZILIAN COFFEE.

C'est toi, divin café, dont l'aimable liqueur,
Sans altérer la tête, épanouit le cœur !
A'pei· e j'ai senti ta vapeur odorante,
Soudain de ton climat ·a chaleur pénétrante
Réveille tous mes sens, sans trouble, sans chaos ;
Mes pensers plus nombreux accourent à grands flots ;
Mon idée était triste, aride, dépouillée,
Elle rit, elle sort richement habillée,
Et je crois, du génie éprouvant le réveil,
Boire dans chaque goutte un rayon du soleil !
*—*Delille.

COFFEE.

ITS PRODUCTION.

L' immense développement de la culture du café au Brésil et la rapidité du mouvement, surtout dans un pays où les bras sont si rares, sont au nombre des phénomènes économiques de notre siècle les plus frappants. —Agassiz, *Voyage au Brésil.*

The coffee plant or tree, a native of Arabia, has been acclimated in many other countries, and above all in Brazil, where it has found a soil and a climate peculiarly favorable to its culture.

The world's total annual production is estimated at 666,000,000 kilogrammes, of which 360,000,000 are produced by Brazil.

It will thus be seen that Brazil furnishes more than one-half the entire production of the globe ; and we may add that its production in that country is rapidly extending and increasing, while almost everywhere else it is diminishing.

For twenty years past the Brazilian planters have taken pains to plant only the best kinds of coffee, to adopt the best methods of cultivation, and employ the most improved machinery ; and their intelligent efforts have been rewarded by the excellent quality of their productions. In more than twenty expositions in the last three years, the coffees of Brazil have obtained the preference over all those from other countries, and have everywhere the highest distinctions, gold medals and diplomas.

In a word, Brazil is by far the leading producer of coffee, both as regards quantity and quality.

ITS UTILITY.

Coffee, which makes the politician wise,
And see through all things with his half-shut eyes.
—Pope.

Coffee furnishes a beverage not only agreeable, but also healthful, tonic, and possessing anti-febrile properties, which regulates digestion and sustains the physical forces, while at the same time imparting animation and keenness to the intellectual faculties.

The consumption of coffee in hot countries is enormous, because there it takes the place of alcoholic drinks, whose abuse would be deadly ; and in cold regions its use is increasing and spreading more and more, because there it warms and strengthens like brandy, without its bad effects. Quite to the contrary, coffee taken with brandy enhances the good effects of the alcohol, while lessening the dreadful consequences resulting from its abuse.

The experience of recent wars has confirmed the useful effects of coffee, and shown that it may be employed with vast benefit in the alimentation of armies in the field.

Coffee is destined to occupy a constantly increasing place in the consumption of all nations, and Brazil, which possesses more than three million square kilometres of land suited to its culture, will be able to increase its production to meet the demands of the increasing consumption.

PREPARATION OF THE COFFEE.

Que j'aime à préparer ton nectar précieux!
Nul n'usurpe chez moi ce soin délicieux.
— DELILLE.

We are not going to speak here of the care to be taken by the producer, and the handling of the grain, until it is put in bags and sent to market; we intend merely to give the consumer the directions which are indispensable for him who would have good coffee.

It is important to know that green, that is, unroasted coffee, improves with age, if kept in a dry place. *Coffee, like bottled wine, improves as it grows older;* but, as in growing older, it grows drier, it necessarily loses in weight, while it increases in price; and the result of this is, that only young coffees are to be found in the market, whose aroma has not completely developed.

Wealthy lovers of coffee should keep their coffee in the store-room, like their wine in the cellar, and be able to offer their guests a cup of coffee of six or eight years of age, or even older.

In regard to the sort to select and the mixture to make, that must depend on individual taste; but we may mention here that Brazil has, upon its immense territory, adopted and acclimated all the known varieties, old and new; and that more than one-half the coffees sold as Moka, Java, Martinique, Bourbon, etc., are in reality Brazilian coffees.

Once arrived at the desired age, the question arises, how to *roast* the coffee. This is a delicate operation, demanding great care and attention. If badly done, the coffee will preserve a disagreeable raw taste, if roasted too little; or a portion of the aroma will be lost, and a part of the coffee changed to charcoal, if roasted too much. Further, the outside of the grain may be burnt and carbonized, while the inside remains raw; or the roasting may be so uneven as to leave some of the grains still raw, while others are burnt.

These consequences may be avoided by placing the roaster over a fire not too hot, in order that the heat may have time to reach the interior of the grains, and roast that part, without burning the outside, by turning the roaster constantly and regularly, so that the heat, being evenly distributed through the whole mass, may roast it evenly; finally, by opening the roaster from time to time to ascertain the progress of the roasting. As soon as the grains become of deep chestnut color, the coffee is sufficiently roasted.

The roasted coffee should be used at once, or should not be kept more than two or three days at most; as, after that time, an essential oil is secreted, which oxidizes in contact with the air, and becomes rancid like butter. We therefore advise those who roast their coffee at home, to roast only small quantities at a time; and those who buy their coffee already roasted, to buy it at houses that sell great quantities, and never sell except the freshly roasted.

For a still stronger reason, coffee should only be ground just before it is needed, for in the powder it loses its aroma rapidly. One should never buy ground coffee at the grocer's, not alone because of the loss of aroma, but also and especially of the adulterations of all sorts to which ground coffee is exposed. Every family should have its own little coffee-mill, and grind every time only the quantity needed. All sorts of coffee-pots may be used, but those of porcelain, earthenware, silver or britannia, are to be preferred. Ground coffee should be placed in the filter or strainer-bag, so that the upper surface shall be level; otherwise the water will not pass equally through the powder, and, consequently, will not extract all its strength. The water should be poured on boiling, little by little, up to the quantity required, in order that the powder may have time to become thoroughly steeped, and give up to the water all the soluble parts, which constitute the strength and aroma of the beverage.

When this is done, the coffee is ready to be served. Care should be taken *that the coffee does not boil*, as by so doing it loses its flavor. If it be not drunk while it is yet hot, it is better not to heat it again, but to drink it cold.

— J. DUMONTIER, Ex-Chief of Battalion of Engineers,
Secretary of the Brazilian Commission at the Exposition of St. Petersburg.

. . . . . Cette liqueur au poète si chère,
Qui manquait à Virgile et qu'adorait Voltaire.
— DELILLE.

"It was my desire to become acquainted with the facts connected with coffee culture in Brazil during the past fifty years. The immense and rapid development of this branch of industry, above all in a country where labor is scarce, is one of the economic phenomena, the most impressive of our century. Thanks to their perseverance and the favorable conditions of soil, the Brazilians have acquired almost a monopoly in coffee, since *more than half of the world's consumption is of Brazilian production.* And in spite of this, the reputation of Brazilian coffee is low, and it is quoted at a lower price than others. And for what reason? Simply because a great part of the better sorts produced on Brazilian plantations is sold in the markets under the name of Java, Moka, Martinique and Bourbon. Now, the amount exported annually by Martinique is 600 bags; Guadalupe, whose coffee bears the name of its sister isle, produces 6,000 bags per annum—not enough to supply the Rio market for twenty-four hours;* the Isle of Bourbon furnishes scarcely more. Nearly all the coffee sold under these different names, and sometimes under that of Java, comes from Brazil, and the so-called *Moka* is often nothing but the small, round grains from Brazilian plantations."
— Professor AGASSIZ, of the United States, "*Voyage to Brazil.*"

"Brazilian coffee is superior to that of other countries in the amount of caffeine which it contains."
— Dr. E. LUDWIG, Chief of the Laboratory of Chemistry of the Faculty of Medicine of Vienna.

"All hygienists are to-day agreed in recognizing the healthful and stimulating properties of coffee, and in the desire to see it take a place of increasing importance among the alimentary substances. The experience of recent wars, and particularly that of our army in Africa, have shown so clearly the benefits of the use of this tonic that its

* The annual production of Brazil is 6,000,000 bags of 60 kilos. each.

61

use has become official in the army, when the soldier is exposed to fatigues or special unhealthful influences. The use of coffee as a morning beverage has happily already widely spread among the laboring population, and seems likely to take the place, with happy results, of the habit of drinking brandy, before commencing the labor of the day— a habit whose effects upon the organism are so pernicious.

"In short, apart from the coffees of Arabia, Martinique and Reunion, which together form less than 6 per cent. of the consumption of France, *it is the Brazilian coffees which deserve the preference in our commerce, not only on account of the care given to their cultivation and gathering, but still more on account of their good quality.*"

—GENERAL MORIN, Directeur du Conservatoire des Arts-et-Métiers de Paris,

Annales du Conservatoire des A. et M.

"*The Brazilian coffee is confessedly one of the best.* Speculators have resorted to subterfuge and enriched themselves at the expense of the coffee of Brazil, by selling it under the name of Moka and Martinique, and sometimes as Ceylon, Java or Reunion. This fraud has been successful, for its qualities were such as to favor the falsification; and what speaks still more loudly in its favor is the fact that it has successfully contested the field with the coffee of Yemen even, on the very spot of its production and commerce."

—M. CALLIMAN, *French Economist.*

"The general use of coffee is one of the elements of civilization, and one may judge of the temperance of a people by the amount of coffee which they drink. Why not make the use of black coffee after meal obligatory, in educational establishments? Healthful, of a delicious perfume and agreeable flavor, it is also, through its hydrocarbon elements, a superior respiratory aliment. Through its nitrogenous principles, caffeine, without being positively nutritious, supports the organism, stimulates it, and aids in a marked manner the functions of digestion. It never produces depression, which is the secondary effect of alcoholic stimulants."

—BARON DE THERESOPOLIS, Discourse at the "Congrès International d'Hygiène et de Démographie à Genève," 1883.

"The suppression of alcoholic drinks can be effected only by substituting for it a liquid possessing the same properties without leaving the same wretched effects. Coffee is truly indispensable to soldiers, as it not only sustains, arouses and stimulates them, but more important still, preserves them from, or cures them of, a disease quite frequent in armies in campaign or on the march—diarrhœa. Coffee is the best hygienic agent of prevention."

DR. LUCIEN MARTIN, *Journal d'Hygiène Pratique.*

EXHIBIT OF COFFEE

MADE BY THE ASSOCIATION

CENTRO DA LAVOURA E COMMERCIO OF RIO DE JANEIRO,

—: AT THE :—

WORLD'S INDUSTRIAL AND COTTON CENTENNIAL EXPOSITION

OF NEW ORLEANS.

List of Exhibitors of Coffee from Brazil at the World's Industrial and Cotton Centennial Exposition of New Orleans.

No.	NAME OF EXHIBITOR.	MUNICIPIUM AND PROVINCE	QUALITY.
1	Marianna Leite & Genro	Valença, Rio de Janeiro	Washed, regular, 1.
2	Carlos Burgués	Cantagallo, Rio de Janeiro	Washed, good, 1.
3	Lieutenant-Colonel Antonio Furtado de Campos	Pomba, Minas Geraes	1st regular, 2.
4	Francisco Marcondes Machado	Sapucaia, Rio de Janeiro	1st good, 1.
5	Mauricio Haritoff	Pirahy, Rio de Janeiro	Superior, 1.
6	Baron de Santa Leocadia	Rio Novo, Minas Geraes	Superior, 2.
7	Heirs of João Pereira da Silva	Valença, Rio de Janeiro	Washed, superior, 2.
8	Francisca da Cunha Nobrega Ayrosa	Juiz de Fora, Minas Geraes	Washed, regular, 1.
9	Ang-lica de Souza Araujo	Sapucaia, Rio de Janeiro	Washed, good, 2.
10	Antonio Pinto Vieira	Carmo, Rio de Janeiro	Washed, regular, 1.
11	Antonio dos Santos Lima Thompson	Cantagallo, Rio de Janeiro	Washed, regular, 2.
12	Commander Joaquim de Campos Negreiros	Leopoldina, Minas Geraes	1st good, 2.
13	Bernardo Belizario Soares de Souza	S. José d'Alem Parahyba, Minas Geraes.	1st good, 2.
14	Heirs of Manoel Antonio Esteves	Valença, Rio de Janeiro	Washed, good, 1.
15	Lieutenant-Colonel Manoel Gomes Vieira & Filho	Taubaté, S. Paulo	Washed, round, 2.
16	Pedro José Henriques	Juiz de Fora, Minas Geraes	Round, 2.
17	Baroness de S. José do Rio Preto	Juiz de Fora, Minas Geraes	Round, 4.
18	Commander Luiz Caetano Alves	Vassouras, Rio de Janeiro	1st good, 2.
19	Mello & Irmãos	Cantagallo, Rio de Janeiro	1st good, 2.
20	Antonio Lopes do Babo	Parahyba do Sul, Rio de Janeiro	1st good, 1.
21	Captain Manoel Goulart de Souza	Carmo, Rio de Janeiro	1st good, 2.
22	Francisco Marcondes Machado	Sapucaia, Rio de Janeiro	1st good, 2.
23	Angela Penelope de Moraes	Amparo, S. Paulo	Round, 3.
24	Lucas Soares de Gouveia	Leopoldina, Minas Geraes	1st good, 2.
25	Antonio de Souza Alves	Valença, Rio de Janeiro	1st good, 2.
26	Widow and Heirs of M. G. Vieira da Cruz	Parahyba do Sul, Rio de Janeiro	Round, 2.
27	Baron de Itapura	Campinas, S. Paulo	1st good, 2.
28	Baron do Rio Negro	Barra Mansa, Rio de Janeiro	1st regular, 1.
29	Antonio Tertuliano Ribeiro	Juiz de Fora, Minas Geraes	1st good, 1.
30	Heirs of Manoel Antonio Esteves	Valença, Rio de Janeiro	Washed, round, superior, 1.
31	Francisco Clemente Pinto	Cantagallo, Rio de Janeiro	Washed, round, 2.
32	Doctor Vicente Moncada	Cantagallo, Rio de Janeiro	1st good, 2.
33	Widow Teixeira & Filho	Cantagallo, Rio de Janeiro	1st good, 2.
34	Manoel Luiz Alves & Co	Juiz de Fora, Minas Geraes	1st good, 2.
35	José Moreira Marcondes Romeiro & Co	Pindamonhangaba, S. Paulo	1st good, 2.
36	Doctor José Monteiro Machado Cesar	Pindamonhangaba, S. Paulo	1st good, 1.
37	Lacerda Brum & Irmão	Vassouras, Rio de Janeiro	Washed, inferior.
38	Baron de Juiz de Fora	Juiz de Fora, Minas Geraes	1st good, 1.
39	Baron de Itatiaya	Juiz de Fora, Minas Geraes	1st good, 2.
40	Colonel Albino Antonio de Almeida	Rezende, Rio de Janeiro	1st good, 2.
41	Lieutenant Francisco Alvares de Magalhães	S. José de Barreiros, S. Paulo	1st regular, 1.
42	Captain Severino José Henriques	Juiz de Fora, Minas Geraes	Washed, regular, 2.
43	Francisco de Assis Teixeira	Leopoldina, Minas Geraes	1st good, 1.
44	José Leite de Figueiredo	Parahyba do Sul, Rio de Janeiro	1st good, 1.
45	João Alves Constantino	Rio Novo, Minas Geraes	1st good, 1.
46	João Paulo de Castro	Rio Novo, Minas Geraes	1st good, 1.
47	Francisco Paulo de Almeida	Valença, Rio de Janeiro	Washed, superior, 1.
48	Carvalho & Faro	Valença, Rio de Janeiro	Round, 1.
49	Commander Manoel Carlos Aranha	Campinas, S. Paulo	1st good, 2.
50	Miguel José Rodrigues Pereira	Parahyba do Sul, Rio de Janeiro	1st regular, 2.
51	Barros & Santos	Limeira, S. Paulo	Round, 3.
52	João José Vieira	Valença, Rio de Janeiro	1st good, 2.
53	José Francisco Ferreira Guimarães	Vassouras, Rio de Janeiro	Washed, regular, 2.
54	Doctor Antonio Lazzarini	Vassouras, Rio de Janeiro	Washed, fine.
55	Antonio Bernardino Monteiro de Barros	Parahyba do Sul, Rio de Janeiro	1st good, 2.
56	José Ferreira Leite da Silva	Areias, S. Paulo	Washed, regular, 2.
57	Luiza de Avellar Lengruber	Carmo, Rio de Janeiro	Round, 2.
58	Major Lindorf Moreira de Vasconcellos	Vassouras, Rio de Janeiro	1st good, 1.
59	Doctor Joaquim Barbosa de Castro	Mar de Hespanha, Minas Geraes	1st good, 2.
60	Virgilio Rodrigues Alves	Guaratinguetá, S. Paulo	Washed, round, 3.
61	Commander Raymundo de Oliveira Roxo	Vassouras, Rio de Janeiro	1st good, 2.
62	José Augusto de Rezende	Rio Novo, Minas Geraes	1st good, 2.
63	Major José Luiz Rodrigues Horta	Juiz de Fora, Minas Geraes	1st good, 2.
64	Baron de Taubaté	Pindamonhangaba, S. Paulo	1st good, 1.
65	Maria Candida Perpetua	Juiz de Fora, Minas Geraes	1st good, 1.
66	José Pereira dos Santos	S. Paulo	Round, 4.
67	Commander Romualdo José Monteiro de Barros	Pirahy, Rio de Janeiro	1st good, 1.
68	Luiza de Avellar Lengruber	Carmo, Rio de Janeiro	1st good, 1.
69	Estanislau Ferreira de Camargo Andrade	Campinas, S. Paulo	Washed, regular, 1.
70	Antonio José Pereira de Carvalho	Carmo, Rio de Janeiro	Washed, good, 2.
71	José Antonio da Silva	Nova Friburgo, Rio de Janeiro	Washed, regular, 1.
72	Widow and Heirs of Manoel Gomes Vieira da Cruz	Parahyba do Sul, Rio de Janeiro	1st good, 2.

No.	NAME OF EXHIBITOR.	MUNICIPIUM AND PROVINCE.	QUALITY.
73	Baron de Piracicaba	Rio Claro, S. Paulo	Washed, regular, 1.
74	Viscount de Arcozello	Vassouras, Rio de Janeiro	Round, 4.
75	Doctor Thomar de Aquino Leite	Juiz de Fora, Minas Geraes	1st good, 1.
76	Singlehmet & Co	Ceará	Round.
77	Francisco de Paulo Galdino Leite & Filho	Sapucaia, Rio de Janeiro	1st good, 2.
78	Ensign Joaquim José da Silva Leme	Areias, S. Paulo	Washed, regular, 1.
79	Carlos José Ribeiro	Juiz de Fora, Minas Geraes	1st good, 1.
80	Quintiliano & Sobrinho	Vassouras, Rio de Janeiro	1st good, 1.
81	José Leite de Figueiredo	Bananal, S. Paulo	1st good, 1.
82	Firmo Alves Pereira & Filho	Parahyba do Sul, Rio de Janeiro	1st good, 1.
83	Baron de Juiz de Fora	Juiz de Fora, Minas Geraes	1st good, 1.
84	Antonio Tertuliano Ribeiro	Juiz de Fora, Minas Geraes	1st good, 2.
85	Silveira & Sobrinhas	Rezende, Rio de Janeiro	1st good, 1.
86	Joaquim de Paula Souza Camargo	Amparo, S. Paulo	1st good, 1.
87	Cornelio de Souza Lima	Sta. Maria Magdalena, Rio de Janeiro	1st good, 1.
88	Luiz Pereira de Faro	Vassouras, Rio de Janeiro	1st good, 2.
89	Luiz Ribeiro da Silva	Cantagallo, Rio de Janeiro	Washed, good, 2.
90	Viscount de S. Clemente	Cantagallo, Rio de Janeiro	Washed, fine.
91	Viscount de Indaiatuba	Campinas, S. Paulo	Round, 1.
92	Salathiel de Faria Lobato & Co	Mar de Hespanha, Minas Geraes	Round, 2.
93	Baron do Rio Bonito	Valença, Rio de Janeiro	Round, 2.
94	Heirs of A gusto Perret	Vassouras, Rio de Janeiro	Washed, regular, 2.
95	Baron de Avellar e Almeida	Vassouras, Rio de Janeiro	1st good, 1.
96	Viscount de Arcozello	Vassouras, Rio de Janeiro	Washed, superior, 2.
97	Baron de Cantagallo	Cantagallo, Rio de Janeiro	Washed, good, 2.
98	Doctor José Pereira Leite e Silva	Rezende, Rio de Janeiro	Washed, regular, 2.
99	Eduardo Carneiro de Mendonça	Mar de Hespanha, Minas Geraes	Washed, regular 2.
100	Barbosa Lima & Filho	Rezende, Rio de Janeiro	Washed, inferior.
101	Doctor José Bernardo Gomes Guimarães	Barra Mansa, Rio de Janeiro	Round, 1.
102	Francisco Silveira da Cunha	Rezende, Rio de Janeiro	1st good, 1.
103	João Antonio Dias	Vassouras, Rio de Janeiro	Washed, superior, 1.
104	Commander Lucas Antonio Monteiro de Barros	Pirahy, Rio de Janeiro	Round, 3.
105	Baron de Santa Maria	Vassouras, Rio de Janeiro	Washed, good, 2.
106	Cherubina Maria Ribeiro	Nova Friburgo, Rio de Janeiro	Washed, regular.
107	Salathiel de Faria Lobato & Co	Mar de Hespanha, Minas Geraes	1st good, 1.
108	Araujo Maia & Irmão	S. João Nepomuceno, Minas Geraes	Washed, regular. 1.
109	José de Lacerda Guimarães	Araras, S. Paulo	Washed, round, 3.
110	Francisco Querino da Rocha Werneck	Parahyba do Sul, Rio de Janeiro	1st good, 1.
111	Modesto Henrique de Mattos	Mar de Hespanha, Minas Geraes	Round, 3.
112	Doctor Raphael Aguiar Paes de Barros	Pirassununga, S. Paulo	Washed, regular, 1.
113	Commander Romualdo José Monteiro de Barros	Pirahy, Rio de Janeiro	Round, 2.
114	Marchioness de Paraná	Sapucaia, Rio de Janeiro	Washed, regular, 2.
115	Colonel Antonio Luiz da Silveira	Pirahy, Rio de Janeiro	1st regular, 1.
116	Lieutenant-Colonel Antonio José Barbosa de Andrade	Parahyba do Sul, Rio de Janeiro	Washed, good, 1.
117	Doctor Leandro Dezerra Monteiro	Parahyba do Sul, Rio de Janeiro	Washed, regular, 1.
118	Baron de Cananéa	Vassouras, Rio de Janeiro	1st good, 1.
119	Commander Pompeu Augusto Cezar da Costa	Santo Antonio de Padua, Rio de Janeiro	Round, 3.
120	Luiz Ribeiro da Cunha	Ceará	Round.
121	Captain Lucio Correia e Castro	Parahyba do Sul, Rio de Janeiro	Round, 4.
122	Araujo Maia & Irmão	S. João Nepomuceno, Minas Geraes	Washed, round, 2.
123	Manoel Gonçalves Barroso	S. João Nepomuceno, Minas Geraes	1st ordinary, 2.
124	Marinho & Irmão	Sapucaia, Rio de Janeiro	Washed, good. 2.
125	Major Francisco Pereira Ramos	Rezende, Rio de Janeiro	Washed, good, 2.
126	Heirs of Manoel Antonio Esteves	Valença, Rio de Janeiro	Washed, special.
127	Baron de Santa Fé	Valença, Rio de Janeiro	Washed, regular, 2.
128	Commander Francisco Ferreira de Assis Fonseca	Juiz de Fora, Minas Geraes	Washed, regular, 2.
129	Mauricio Haritoff	Pirahy, Rio de Janeiro	Round, 1.
130	Doctor Manoel Simões de Souza Pinto	Leopoldina, Minas Geraes	Washed regular, 1.
131	João José Pereira da Silva	Valença, Rio de Janeiro	Washed, good, 1.
132	Doctor Antonio Lazzarini	Vassouras, Rio de Janeiro	Washed, fine.
133	A. Ermelindo Ribeiro	Valença, Rio de Janeiro	Superior, 2.
134	Doctor Thomaz Vieira de Freitas	Sapucaia, Rio de Janeiro	Round, 1.
135	Carvalho & Faro	Valença, Rio de Janeiro	Washed, fine.
136	Lieutenant-Colonel Antonio José Barbosa de Andrade	Parahyba do Sul, Rio de Janeiro	Washed, good, 2.
137	Dietrick & Cunhados	Cantagallo, Rio de Janeiro	Washed, regular, 1.
138	Antonio Augusto Monteiro de Barros	Limeira, S. Paulo	Washed, regular, 1.
139	Thomaz Ignacio Botelho	Juiz de Fora, Minas Geraes	1st regular, 1.
140	Florentino Mariano dos Santos	Parahyba do Sul, Rio de Janeiro	1st regular, 2.
141	Anna da Cunha Ferreira Carneiro	Juiz de Fora, Minas Geraes	Superior, 2.
142	Araujo Maia & Irmão	S. João Nepomuceno, Minas Geraes	1st regular, 1.
143	João Domingues dos Santos	Juiz de Fora, Minas Geraes	1st regular, 2.
144	J. M. Machado	Vassouras, Rio de Janeiro	Fine.
145	José Maria Machado	Vassouras, Rio de Janeiro	1st ordinary, 1.
146	Jeronymo Francisco Ascenso Duraes	S. Matheus, Espirito Santo	2d good, 1.
147	Antonio Alves Pinto da Cruz	Rio Preto, Minas Geraes	1st regular, 2.
148	Viscount de S. Clemente	Cantagallo, Rio de Janeiro	Washed, superior. 1.
149	Cecilia Maria de Jesus Nobrega	Pirahy, Rio de Janeiro	1st regular, 2.
150	Antonio P. dos Santos Rezende	Leopoldina, Minas Geraes	2d good, 1.
151	Maria Justina da Purificação	Cantagallo, Rio de Janeiro	1st ordinary, 2.
152	Anna de Pontes França & Irmão	Juiz de Fora, Minas Geraes	1st ordinary, 2.
153	Viscount de Nova Friburgo	Cantagallo, Rio de Janeiro	Washed, round, 3.
154	Bicudo & Irmão	Campinas, S. Paulo	Round, 1.
155	Guilherme Sauerbrown	Cantagallo, Rio de Janeiro	1st regular, 1.
156	Domiciano Esteves dos Santos	Cataguazes, Minas Geraes	2d good, 2.
157	Antoni Luiz Machado	Sapucaia, Rio de Janeiro	2d good, 2.
158	Joséo Teixeira Portugal Freixe	Sta. Maria Magdalena, Rio de Janeiro	1st ordinary, 2.

No.	NAME OF EXHIBITOR.	MUNICIPIUM AND PROVINCE.	QUALITY.
159	Joaquim Candido Guimarães	Rio Preto, Minas Geraes	1st regular, 1.
160	Manoel Joaquim da Rocha	Leopoldina, Minas Geraes	1st ordinary, 1.
161	Marciano Furtado de Mendonça	S. João Nepomuceno, Minas Geraes	1st regular, 2.
162	Lieutenant Fortunato José Pereira de Souza	Rio Novo, Minas Geraes	1st ordinary, 1.
163	Matheus X. Monteiro Nogueira da Gama	Itapemerim, Espirito Santo	2d ordinary.
164	Carolina Josepha da Silva Vieira	Valença, Rio de Janeiro	1st regular, 1.
165	Antonio Loureiro Caldas	Parahyba do Sul, Rio de Janeiro	1st regular, 1.
166	Doctor Galdino Antonio do Valle	Sta. Maria Magdalena, Rio de Janeiro	1st regular, 2.
167	Captain Pedro Augusto de Lacerda	Vassouras, Rio de Janeiro	1st good, 1.
168	Luiz Pereira Romeu	Parahyba do Sul, Rio de Janeiro	1st ordinary, 2.
169	Baron de Itapeba	Pindamonhangaba, S. Paulo	1st regular, 1.
170	Antonio José dos Santos Nazareth	Juiz de Fora, Minas Geraes	1st ordinary, 2.
171	Marianna Leite & Genro	Valença, Rio de Janeiro	Washed superior, 2.
172	Joaquim Manoel Alves	S. Paulo	1st regular, 1.
173	Lieutenant Valeriano C. dos Santos Monteiro	Leopoldina, Minas Geraes	2d ordinary.
174	Manoel Gomes Leal do Nascimento	Barra Mansa, Rio de Janeiro	1st ordinary, 1.
175	Antonio de Souza Lima Niquinho	Santo Antonio de Padua, Rio de Janeiro	1st ordinary, 1.
176	Doctor Antonio Justiniano das Chagas & Co	Mar de Hespanha, Minas Geraes	1st good, 2.
177	Baron de Louriçal	Mar de Hespanha, Minas Geraes	1st ordinary, 1.
178	Captain Antonio Manoel Pacheco	Juiz d' Fora, Minas Geraes	1st good, 2.
179	Lucas Antonio Monteiro de Barros	S. José d'Alem Parahyba, Minas Geraes	2d good, 1.
180	Domiciana M. de Almeida Vallim	Bananal, S. Paulo	1st good, 1.
181	Doctor Carlos Theodoro de Bustamante	Barra Mansa, Rio de Janeiro	1st ordinary, 2.
182	José Ignacio Ferreira	Valença, Rio de Janeiro	2d good, 1.
183	Heirs of João Antonio Alves de Brito	Mar de Hespanha, Minas Geraes	1st ordinary, 2.
184	Carvalho & Co	Barra Mansa, Rio de Janeiro	1st ordinary, 1.
185	Modesto Henrique de Mattos	Mar de Hespanha, Minas Geraes	1st ordinary, 2.
186	Joaquim Candido Guimarães	Rio Preto, Minas Geraes	1st regular, 2.
187	Luiz Teixeira de Barros	Pindamonhangaba, S. Paulo	1st regular, 1.
188	Department of Public Lands and Colonisation	Colony Santa Isabel, Espirito Santo	2d good, 2.
189	Baron do Rio Negro	Barra Mansa, Rio de Janeiro	1st regular, 1.
190	Saturnino Dias Telles de Castro	Queluz, S. Paulo	1st regular, 1.
191	Tristão Correia Dias	Leopoldina, Minas Geraes	2d good, 2.
192	José Botelho Ferreira Bezerra	Cantagallo, Rio de Janeiro	2d good, 2.
193	Placido José de Almeida	Valença, Rio de Janeiro	2d good, 1.
194	Joaquim Vieira da Silva Rezende	Cataguazes, Minas Geraes	1st regular, 1.
195	Commander Luiz Antonio da Costa e Souza	Pirahy, Rio de Janeiro	1st ordinary, 1.
196	Antonio Crispim de Abreu	Pirassununga, S. Paulo	1st regular, 1.
197	Joaquim José de Carvalho Lima & Irmãos	Parahyba do Sul, Rio de Janeiro	1st ordinary, 1.
198	Casemiro Antonio Vidal	Minas Geraes	1st ordinary, 1.
199	Commander João Nogueira de Mattos	Taubaté, S. Paulo	2d good, 1.
200	Doctor José Bernardo Gomes Guimarães	Barra Mansa, Rio de Janeiro	1st regular, 2.
201	Luiz Ribeiro da Cunha	Ceará	Special.
202	Maria Francisca Kemistz de Lima	Juiz de Fora, Minas Geraes	1st ordinary, 2.
203	Doctor Candido Ferreira da Silva Camargo	Campinas, S. Paulo	1st regular, 2.
204	Maria Clara Lopes Martins	Cantagallo, Rio de Janeiro	1st ordinary, 2.
205	Manoel Joaquim Marques Melgaço	Sapucaia, Rio de Janeiro	1st ordinary, 1.
206	Lieutenant-Colonel Fabiano Martins Alves Porto, Jr	Jacarehy, S. Paulo	1st regular, 1.
207	Francisco Jacintho da Silva	Sta. Maria Magdalena, Rio de Janeiro	2d good, 1.
208	João Pires da Veiga	Cantagallo, Rio de Janeiro	1st ordinary, 1.
209	Francisco Angelo Correia	Sapucaia, Rio de Janeiro	1st regular, 1.
210	Mathias Octavio Roxo	Pirahy, Rio de Janeiro	1st regular, 1.
211	Joaquim Candido de Almeida Leite	Belem do Descalvado, S. Paulo	1st regular, 2.
212	Manoel Dias da Cunha	Pirahy, Rio de Janeiro	2d good, 1.
213	Maria Bussinger Bon	Cantagallo, Rio de Janeiro	2d good, 1.
214	Augusto Mendes Ferreira	Rio Novo, Minas Geraes	1st regular, 1.
215	José de Souza Campos	Campinas, S. Paulo	1st regular, 1.
216	José Augusto de Figueiredo Cortes	S. José d'Alem Parahyba, Minas Geraes	1st regular, 1.
217	Colonel Mariano José de Oliveira e Costa	Taubaté, S. Paulo	1st regular, 1.
218	José Cesario de Figueiredo Cortes	Leopoldina, Minas Geraes	1st regular, 1.
219	Colonel João Gomes de Aguiar	Parahyba do Sul, Rio de Janeiro	1st ordinary, 1.
220	State of Julio Leite Ribeiro	Santo Antonio de Padua, Rio de Janeiro	2d good, 1.
221	Braz Marcondes de Toledo	Barra Mansa, Rio de Janeiro	1st ordinary, 1.
222	Major Antonio Pereira Baptista	Areias, S. Paulo	1st regular, 1.
223	Venancio José Garcia	S. Fidelis, Rio de Janeiro	2d good, 1.
224	Antonio José Luiz	Barra Mansa, Rio de Janeiro	1st regular, 2.
225	José Rebello da Silva	S. Fidelis, Rio de Janeiro	1st ordinary, 1.
226	Victorino Joaquim Monteiro	Muriahé, Minas Geraes	2d good, 2.
227	Commander Francisco José de Carvalho	Valença, Rio de Janeiro	1st regular, 2.
228	Francisco Pinheiro de Lacerda	Cantagallo, Rio de Janeiro	1st ordinary, 1.
229	Eugenio Julio Curty	Cantagallo, Rio de Janeiro	1st ordinary, 1.
230	Francisco Avelino do Nascimento	Pindamonhangaba, S. Paulo	1st ordinary, 1.
231	Widow and Sons of Simeão G. da Assumpção	Valença, Rio de Janeiro	1st regular, 1.
232	Antonio Emilio de Abreu	Cantagallo, Rio de Janeiro	2d good, 2.
233	Francisco Machado de Magalhães	Ponte Nova, Minas Geraes	1st good, 2.
234	Antonio Leite de Carvalho e Silva	Mar de Hespanha, Minas Geraes	2d good, 2.
235	Antonio José Paulino	Parahyba do Sul, Rio de Janeiro	1st regular, 1.
236	Manoel José Pereira Torres	S. José d'Alem Parahyba, Minas Geraes	1st regular, 1.
237	Doctor Joseph Lynch	Ubá, Minas Geraes	1st regular, 1.
238	Maria de Figueiredo Freire	Sta. Maria Magdalena, Rio de Janeiro	1st ordinary, 1.
239	Francisco Diocleciano Ribeiro	Pirassununga, S. Paulo	1st regular, 1.
240	Francisco de Faria Salgado	Cantagallo, Rio de Janeiro	1st regular, 1.
241	João Albino Dias da Silva	Cantagallo, Rio de Janeiro	1st regular, 1.
242	José Joaquim Pereira Ramos	Cataguazes, Minas Geraes	2d good, 1.
243	José Joaquim de Muros	Macahé, Rio de Janeiro	2d good, 1.
244	Rozendo Pereira Salgado	Pindamonhangaba, S. Paulo	2d good, 1.

No.	NAME OF EXHIBITOR.	MUNICIPIUM AND PROVINCE.	QUALITY.
245	Francisco Antunes Pereira	Leopoldina, Minas Geraes	1st ordinary, 1.
246	Captain Francisco Antonio Gonçalves Barbosa	Parahyba do Sul, Rio de Janeiro	1st regular, 2.
247	João Batalha Rodrigues	Muriaé, Minas Geraes	3d good, 1.
248	José Gonçalves V riato de Medeiros	Parahyba do Sul, Rio de Janeiro	1st ordinary, 2.
249	Brandão & Co	Rio Preto, Minas Geraes	1st ordinary. 2
250	Commander Geraldo de Rezende	Campinas, S. Paulo	Washed, good, 2.
251	Antonio Luiz Pinheiro	Cantagallo, Rio de Janeiro	Superior, 1.
252	Francisco Marc ndes Machado	Cantagallo, Rio de Janeiro	Superior, 1.
253	Antonio de Paula Souza	Sapucaia, Rio de Janeiro	Round, 3.
254	José Joaquim Rodrigues	Amparo, S. Paulo	Round, 3.
255	Antonio Carlos de Alvarenga	Nova Friburgo, Rio de Janeiro	Washed, good, 2.
256	Antonio Monteiro dos Santos, Jr	Taubaté, S. Paulo	1st ordinary, 1.
257	Joaquim Ramos da Cruz	Vassouras, Rio de Janeiro	2d good, 1.
258	Francisco da Silva Leite & Irmão	Mar de Hespanha, Minas Geraes	2d good, 1.
259	Antonio Estevam da Cunha	S. José d'Alem Parahyba, Minas Geraes	1st ordinary, 1.
260	Maria José de Nazareth	Barra Mansa, Rio de Janeiro	1st ordina y, 1.
261	Colonel Antonio Luiz da Silveira	Juiz de Fora, Minas Geraes	1st regular, 1.
262	Doctor Joaquim Ignacio de Mornes	Pirahy, Rio de Janeiro	1st regular, 1.
263	Theophilo Ferreira Henriques	Amparo, S. Paulo	1st regular, 2.
264	Commander Bernard no José Borges	Juiz de Fora, Minas Geraes	1st regular, 3.
265	Colonel José Victor de Souza Meirelles	Cantagallo, Rio de Jaꞓeiro	1st ordinary, 1.
266	Francisco Cefidonio Gomes dos Reis	Pirassununga, S. Paulo	1st regular, 1.
267	José Francisco Jorge	Leopoldina, Minas Geraes	1st ordinary, 1.
268	Oscar Te xeira de Figueiredo Cortes	S. Fidelis, Rio de Janeiro	2d good, 2.
269	Francisco Carvalho de Mattos	S. José d'Alem Parahyba, Minas Geraes	Washed, inferior.
270	Widow of Carvalho Gomes & Genros	Barra Mansa, Rio de Janeiro	Washed, superior, 1.
271	Manoel Luiz Pereira de Andrade	Valença, Rio de Janeiro	Washed, regular, 1.
272	Lieutenant-Colonel Fabiano M. Alves Porto, Jr	Vassouras, Rio de Janeiro	1st good, 2.
273	Lieutenant-Colonel Antonio Furtado de Campos	Jacarehy, S. Paulo	1st regular, 1.
274	Luiz Vieira de Carvalho	Pomba, Minas Geraes	1st regular, 2.
275	Ensign João Bueno Rangel	Cantagallo, Rio de Janeiro	1st regular, 2.
276	João Candido Homem de Azevedo	Rezende, Rio de Janeiro	1st ordinary, 2.
277	Luiz Hohsmeister	Pindamonhangaba, S. Paulo	1st ordinary, 1.
278	Doctor José de Souza Brandão	Colony Sta. Leopoldina, Espirito Santo	"Capitania."
279	Lieutenant-Colonel Wenceslau Fernandes de Carvalho	Sapucaia, Rio de Janeiro	1st regular, 1.
280	Francisco Coelho de Magalhães	Capivary, Rio de Janeiro	1st regular, 2.
281	José Luiz Vieira de Macedo	Cantagallo, Rio de Janeiro	1st ordinary, 1.
282	Captain Raphael Augusto da Fonseca Lontra	Parahybuna, S. Paulo	1st regular, 2.
283	Doctor Martinho da Silva Prado	S. Fidelis, Rio de Janeiro	2d good, 1.
284	Rachel & Banho	Araras, S. Paulo	1st regular, 2.
285	João Pedro Diniz Junqueira	Leopoldina, Minas Geraes	2d good, 1.
286	Baron de Trememhé	Pirahy, Rio de Janeiro	Washed, superior, 2.
287	Heirs of Manoel Antonio Esteves	Taubaté, S. Paulo	Washed good, 1.
288	Captain Laureano Rodrigues de Andrade	Valença, Rio de Janeiro	Round, 1.
289	Captain José Ignacio de Avellar Werneck	Parahyba do Sul, Rio de Janeiro	Washed, good, 2.
290	Baron de Oliveira Roxo	Parahyba do Sul, Rio de Janeiro	Washed, good, 1.
291	Francisco Paulo de Almeida	Pirahy, Rio de Janeiro	Round, 2.
292	Viscount de Nova Friburgo	Valença, Rio de Janeiro	Washed, superior, 1
293	Thomaz José Candido Laranja	Cantagallo, Rio de Janeiro	Fine.
294	Mario de Lellis e Silva	Juiz de Fora, Minas Geraes	Superior, 1.
295	Lieutenant Eleuterio Alves Barbosa e Silva	Valença, Rio de Janeiro	Superior, 2.
296	Viscount de S. Clemente	Rezende, Rio de Janeiro	Round, 4.
297	Commander Domingos Theodor de Azevedo, Jr	Cantagallo, Rio de Janeiro	1st good, 1.
298	Doctor Antonio Lazzarini	Valença, Rio de Janeiro	Washed regular, 2.
299	Major Francisco Mariano Halfeld	Vassouras, Rio de Janeiro	Washed, round, special.
300	João Guedes da Costa	Juiz de Fora, Minas Geraes	Superior, 2.
301	Baron de Joatinga	Leopoldina. Minas Geraes	1st good, 2.
302	Viscount de Nova Friburgo	Bananal, S. Paulo	1st good, 2.
303	Colonel Thomé Dias dos Santos Brandão	Cantagallo, Rio de Janeiro	Washed, special.
304	Alfredo Carlos de Avellar	Rio Preto, Minas Geraes	1st regular, 2.
305	Doctor Francisco Leite Ribeiro Guimarães	Vassouras, Rio de Janeiro	1st good, 2.
3 ꞌ6	Joaquim Paulino de Souza Aranha	Pirassununga, S. Paulo	Superior, 1.
3 7	Doctor Antonio Moreira de Castilho	Campinas, S. Paulo	Round, 3.
3 ꞌ8	Antonio Augusto Monteiro de Barros	Parahyba do Sul, Rio de Janeiro	Round, 1.
309	Julio Cesar de Castro	Limeira, S. Paulo	Washed, inferior.
310	Tito Livio Martins	Rio Novo, Minas Geraes	1st good, 1.
311	Baron de Rio Bonito	Rezende, Rio de Janeiro	Round, 1.
312	Bernardino José Borges	Valença, Rio de Janeiro	Washed, special.
313	Colonel Marcellino de Brito Pereira Andrade	Cantagallo, Rio de Janeiro	1st regular, 2.
314	José Tavares da Silva	Juiz de Fora, Minas Geraes	Washed, regular, 1.
315	Manoel Luiz Pereira de Andrade	Valença, Rio de Janeiro	Washed, regular, 1.
316	Maria Clementina Magalhães Pereira	Vassouras, Rio de Janeiro	Round, 2.
317	Viscount de Nova Friburgo	S. José do Barreiro, S. Paulo	Washed, round, 2.
318	Francisco Pompeu do Amaral	Cantagallo, Rio de Janeiro	Washed, superior, 2.
319	Councillor Martinho Alvares da Silva Campos	Campinas, S. Paulo	Washed, round, 3.
320	Manoel Joaquim da Rocha	Parahyba do Sul, Rio de Janeiro	Round, 4.
321	Eduardo Carneiro de Mendonça	Leopoldina, Minas Geraes	Round, 2.
322	Maria dos Anjos Sanches de Paiva	Mar de Hespanha, Minas Geraes	Washed, regular, 2.
323	Jus ino Barbosa da Cruz	Valença, Rio de Janeiro	Superior, 1.
324	José Leite de Figueiredo	Cantagallo Rio de Janeiro	1st good, 2.
325	Joaquim Franco de Camargo, Jr	Bananal, S. Paulo	Round, 3.
326	Commander Geraldo de Rezende	Araras, S. Paulo	Washed, regular, 1.
327	Francisco Soares de Gouveia	Campinas, S. Paulo	Washed, regular, 1.
328	Antonio Lutterback	Sapucaia, Rio de Janeiro	1st good, 2.
329	Francisco Clemente Pinto	Cantagallo, Rio de Janeiro	1st good, 1.
330	Lieutenant-Colonel José Ribeiro da Motta Paes	Pinhal, S. Paulo	Washed, regular, 2.

No.	NAME OF EXHIBITOR.	MUNICIPIUM AND PROVINCE.	QUALITY.
331	Luiz Soares de Gouveia ...	Sapucaia, Rio de Janeiro...	Superior, 1.
332	Mario de Lellis e Silva...	Valença, Rio de Janeiro...	Round, 1.
333	Major Francisco Mariano Halfeld ...	Juiz de Fora, Minas Geraes...	Superior, 2.
334	Antonio Augusto Monteiro de Barros ...	Limeira, S. Paulo ...	Washed, round, 3.
335	Lieutenant-Colonel José Manoel de Aguirra...	Rio Claro, S. Paulo ...	Round, 3.
336	José Antero Roxo ...	Vassouras, Rio de Janeiro...	Washed, round, 2.
337	Doctor Christovam Rodrigues de Andrade...	Parahyba do Sul, Rio de Janeiro...	Washed, good, 2.
338	Emiliano Ferreira Pinto...	Cantagallo, Rio de Janeiro. ...	2d good 1.
339	Captain José Vieira dos Santos Werneck ...	Parahyba do Sul, Rio de Janeiro...	1st good, 2.
340	Custodio de Souza Pinto...	Pirahy, Rio de Janeiro...	Washed, round, 1.
341	Baron de Itatiba....	Campinas, S. Paulo...	Washed, round, 2.
342	José Antero Roxo...	Vassouras, Rio de Janeiro...	Washed, regular, 1.
343	Oliveira Carcez & Irmão...	Queluz, S. Paulo...	Washed, superior, 2.
344	Baron de Piracicaba...	Rio Claro, S. Paulo...	Washed, good, 2.
345	Matheus Gomes do Val...	Valença, Rio de Janeiro...	Round, 1.
346	Léon Perissé & Irmão...	Carmo, Rio de Janeiro...	Washed, good, 2.
347	Manoel Thomaz de Aquino Leite...	Santo Antonio de Padua, Rio de Janeiro...	Round, 3.
348	Doctor Antonio Lazzarini ...	Vassouras, Rio de Janeiro...	Washed, round, 1.
349	Isaias Pereira de Carvalho...	Belem do Descalvado, S. Paulo...	Round, 4.
350	Baron de Oliveira Roxo...	Pirahy, Rio de Janeiro ...	st good, 1.
351	Josué Leite Ribeiro ...	Juiz de Fora, Minas Geraes...	1st good, 2.
352	J. M. de Barros...	Valença, Rio de Janeiro...	Superior, 2.
353	Carlos Justiniano das Chagas & Co...	Juiz de Fora, Minas Geraes....	1st good, 2.
354	Léon Perissé & Irmão...	Carmo, Rio de Janeiro...	1st good, 2.
355	Diniz Junior e Irmão & Quartim...	Sta. Maria Magdalena, Rio de Janeiro ...	Washed, regular, 1.
356	Commander Domingos Theodoro de Azevedo, Jr...	Valença, Rio de Janeiro...	Fine.
357	José Caetano Alves...	Vassouras, Rio de Janeiro...	Washed, good, 2.
358	Commander José Vergueiro...	Limeira, S. Paulo...	Washed, round, special.
359	José Caetano Alves...	Vassouras, Rio de Janeiro...	Washed, good, 2.
360	Commander José Vergueiro...	Limeira, S. Paulo...	Washed, superior, 1.
361	Francisco Ignacio de M. Marcondes...	Pindamonhangaba, S. Paulo...	1st good, 2.
362	Commander Antonio Borges Rodrigues ...	Barra Mansa, Rio de Janeiro...	Washed, good, 2.
363	José Leite de Souza ...	Valença, Rio de Janeiro...	Washed, inferior.
364	Baron de Cantagallo...	Cantagallo, Rio de Janeiro...	Washed, good, 1.
365	Manoel Luiz Pereira de Andrade ...	Vassouras, Rio de Janeiro...	Washed, superior, 1.
366	Valerio Correia Netto ...	Pomba, Minas Geraes...	1st good, 2.
367	Captain Manoel Antonio da Silva Rosa...	Rezende, Rio de Janeiro...	Superior, 2.
368	Baron de S. Carlos	Parahyba do Sul, Rio de Janeiro...	1st ordinary, 1.
369	Doctor João Carlos de Araujo Moreira ...	Ubá, Minas Geraes...	1st good, 2.
370	Honorio Ferreira Pinto ...	Cantagallo, Rio de Janeiro. ...	2d good, 2.
371	Doctor João Baptista de Carvalho...	S. José d'Alem Parahyba, Minas Geraes...	Washed, good, 2.
372	Manoel Joaquim de Souza ...	S. Fidelis, Rio de Janeiro...	Washed, regular, 2.
373	Luiza de Avellar Lengruber...	Carmo, Rio de Janeiro...	1st good, 1.
374	Widow Miranda Jordão & Filho ...	Parahyba do Sul, Rio de Janeiro ...	Superior, 1.
375	Colonel Joaquim Luiz de Souza Breves...	S. José d'Alem Parahyba, Minas Geraes...	1st good, 2.
376	Doctor França Carvalho & Councillor Leoncio de Carvalho	Sapucaia, S. Paulo ...	1st good, 2.
377	Baron de Romeiro...	Pindamonhangaba, S. Paulo ...	Round, 3.
378	Rodolpho das Chagas Andrade & Co ...	Mar de Hespanha, Minas Geraes ...	Superior, 1.
379	Luiz Pereira Romeu...	Parahyba do Sul, Rio de Janeiro...	1st ordinary, 2.
380	Francisco Clemente Pinto...	Cantagallo, Rio de Janeiro...	Washed, good, 1.
381	Domingos José da Silva Monteiro...	Lorena, S. Paulo...	1st good, 2.
382	Commander Geraldo de Rezende...	Campinas, S. Paulo...	Washed, good, 2.
383	Doctor Pedro Dias de Carvalho...	Sapucaia, Rio de Janeiro...	Washed, regular, 1.
384	Baron de Ribeiro Barbosa ...	Bananal, S. Paulo...	1st good, 1.
385	Captain Verissimo Antonio da Silveira ..	S. José d'Alem Parahyba, Minas Geraes...	1st good, 2.
386	Colonel Pereira de Barros & Filho...	Taubaté, S. Paulo ...	Washed, regular. 1.
387	Commander Antonio Borges Rodrigues...	Barra Mansa, Rio de Janeiro...	Washed, round, 2.
388	Viscount de S. Clemente...	Cantagallo, Rio de Janeiro...	Washed, good, 1.
389	Francisco de Assis Pereira de Andrade ...	Mar de Hespanha, Minas Geraes ...	Washed, good, 2.
390	Major Antonio Ferreira de Assis...	Leopoldina, Minas Geraes...	1st good, 2.
391	Viscount de Nova Friburgo...	Cantagallo, Rio de Janeiro...	Washed, good 1.
392	Ensign João Goulart de Souza Sobrinho...	Cantagallo, Rio de Janeiro...	Washed, regular, 2.
393	Anna Candida de Salles ...	Rio Claro, S. Paulo ...	1st regular, 1.
394	Petronilha da Silva Rosa...	Rezende, Rio de Janeiro...	Washed, inferior.
395	Doctor Francisco Leite Ribeiro Guimarães...	Pirassununga, S. Paulo...	Washed, " Botucatú."
396	Baron de Santa Maria...	Vassouras, Rio de Janeiro...	Washed, superior, 1.
397	Carolina de Assis Isabel de Campos ...	Juiz de Fora, Minas Geraes...	1st good, 2.
398	Francisco Marcondes Machado...	Sapucaia, Rio de Janeiro ...	1st good, 1.
399	Barros & Santos...	Limeira, S. Paulo...	Round, 3.
400	Lieutenant-Colonel Antonio Furtado de Campos...	Pomba, Minas Geraes...	1st regular, 2.
401 to 402	} Various planters, crop of 1884...	Rio de Janeiro, Minas Geraes and S. Paulo ...	Washed.
403 to 557	} Various planters, crop of 1884...	Rio de Janeiro, Minas Geraes and S. Paulo ...	Unwashed.
558 to 572	} Various planters, crop of 1884...	Rio de Janeiro, Minas Geraes and S. Paulo ...	Washed.
573 to 624	} Various planters, crop of 1884...	Rio de Janeiro, Minas Geraes and S. Paulo ...	Unwashed.

www.ingramcontent.com/pod-product-compliance
Lightning Source LLC
Chambersburg PA
CBHW032247080426
42735CB00008B/1040